Ten-Minute Plays
VOLUME V
FOR KIDS: DRAMA
10+ Format

Ten-Minute Plays

VOLUME V

FOR KIDS

• • •

DRAMA

10+ Format

YOUNG ACTORS SERIES

Kristen Dabrowski

A Smith and Kraus Book

A Smith and Kraus Book
Published by Smith and Kraus, Inc.
177 Lyme Road, Hanover, NH 03755
www.SmithandKraus.com

First Edition: April 2006
10 9 8 7 6 5 4 3 2 1
Manufactured in the United States of America

Cover and text design by Julia Hill Gignoux, Freedom Hill Design

ISBN 1-57525-438-7
10-Minute Plays for Kids Series ISSN 1553-0477

CONTENTS

TO ALL AT THE CREATIVE ARTS SUMMER CAMP
for sharing your time and your talents

INTRODUCTION

Ten-Minute Plays aims to score on many playing fields. This book contains twelve short plays. Each play then contains two scenes and four monologues. Add it up! That means that this book contains twelve plays, twenty-four scenes, and forty-eight monologues. There's a lot to choose from, but it's not overwhelming. The plays and scenes are marked clearly. Note that the text for the monologues is set in a different typeface. If you are working on a monologue and are not performing the play or scene as a whole, take the time to hear in your mind any additional lines or character responses that you need for the monologue to make sense.

Beat indicates there is a dramatic pause in the action. You will want to consider why the beat is there. Does no one know what to do? Is someone thinking?

Feel free to combine characters (so fewer actors are needed), change a character from male to female (or vice versa), or alter the text in any way that suits you. Be as creative as you like!

For each play, I've included tips for young actors and ideas for playwrights. Here's a guide to the symbols:

    🎭   =   tips for actors

    🖋   =   ideas for playwrights

There's a lot to work with here. Actors, the tips are meant to give you some guidance and information on how to be an even finer actor. Playwrights, I've included a few of my inspirations and invite you to borrow from them to write your own plays.

At the end of each play is a section called "Talk Back!" with discussion questions. These questions are catalysts for class discussions and projects. The plays do not make moral judgments. They are intended to spark students to use their imaginations and create their own code of ethics. Even if you're not in school, "Talk Back!" can give you some additional ideas and interesting subjects to discuss.

Lastly, there are four extras in the Appendix: Character Questionnaire for Actors, Playwright's Checklist, Scene Elements Worksheet, and Exploration Games. Each activity adds dimension and depth to the plays and is intended to appeal to various learning styles.

Enjoy!

Kristen Dabrowski

S'MORES

1F, 11M

WHO

FEMALES	MALES
Mom	Dad
	Dave
	Dodge
	Frank
	Gus
	Kyle
	Max
	Mr. Crumble
	Mr. Nick
	Oliver
	Zak

WHERE In the woods.

WHEN Present day.

☻ Consider the family background of your character so you can understand him or her better.

✎ This play is based on *Oliver Twist* by Charles Dickens. I've made it more modern. Try doing the same thing with another classic story.

Scene 1: Asking

MAX: I'm cold.

BEN: That's because Dave here threw up on the fire.

DAVE: I'm sorry, OK?

KYLE: I'm hungry, too.

MAX: I'm literally starving. Is it time to eat yet, Mr. Crumble?

MR. CRUMBLE: Pass around this cracker.

(KYLE grabs the cracker from MR. CRUMBLE's hands.)

MR. CRUMBLE: Don't be greedy, Kyle!

(KYLE obediently takes a small bite and passes the cracker on to the next kid.)

MR. CRUMBLE: Now what do you say, children?

BOYS: Thank you, Mr. Crumble.

(MR. CRUMBLE takes a step away from the group. He's eating from a big box of crackers.)

DAVE: *(Whispering.)* I'm still hungry.

KYLE: Me, too.

BEN: I dare somebody to say something to Mr. Crumble.

DAVE: No way! He's too mean.

MAX: Chicken!

DAVE: That's right, I am!

BEN: Mr. Crumble is one mean dude.

MAX: Oliver, why don't you say something?

OLIVER: Me?

KYLE: Yeah, that's perfect! He'll never see it coming. You're so quiet. He'll never expect it!

MAX: Look at him, chowing down on the whole box of crackers while we have to share one measly cracker. I can't believe he gets away with it. Someone should stand up to him.

(OLIVER has been gathering his courage. He firmly stands and walks over to MR. CRUMBLE.)

OLIVER: Please, sir, can we have s'mores?

MR. CRUMBLE: S'mores?

OLIVER: Please, sir, can we have s'mores?

MR. CRUMBLE: How dare you? You have a perfectly good cracker to share, boy!

OLIVER: One cracker for all of us isn't enough. And I think you're supposed to have s'mores when you're camping. It's the rules.

MR. CRUMBLE: It's the rules, is it? So you're the expert on the rules. Well, I've got some news for you, boy; you're out of order. And the *rules* say that I can punish you. So prepare to be punished!

MAX: He's going to kill him!

MR. CRUMBLE: Silence! *(Beat.)* I am going to give the rest of you boys another cracker to share. Oliver, you're not going to get any.

(OLIVER breathes a sigh of relief.)

MR. CRUMBLE: But that's not all! Oliver, you are going to sit alone for the rest of the night . . .

(OLIVER breathes a sigh of relief.)

MR. CRUMBLE: . . . in a bear's cave!

(BOYS gasp. OLIVER gulps. MR. CRUMBLE grabs OLIVER by the back of his shirt and drags him off to the mouth of a cave.)

MR. CRUMBLE: Now stay there!

OLIVER: But—

MR. CRUMBLE: No whining! No complaining! I'm doing you a favor! I'm making you understand who's the boss here. I'm making you a man, boy!

OLIVER: But, sir—

MR. CRUMBLE: You are a waste of space, Oliver. In the

morning, if you make it that long, I might come back to get you. Good night, Oliver.

(MR. CRUMBLE eats the last cracker from the box. Then he dumps the leftover crumbs over OLIVER's head.)

MR. CRUMBLE: I hear bears are very fond of crackers.

(MR. CRUMBLE exits. OLIVER hastily tries to eat whatever crumbs he can off of his clothes.)

OLIVER: I am not afraid. I am not afraid. Bears are nice. Bears are sweet. I'm too skinny for a bear to want to eat me. Bears are wild animals. Bears are unpredictable. Bears attack people! I'm getting out of here! But if I get out of here, how will I be able to get home tomorrow? Mr. Crumble won't know where I am. Then again, he said he might not come back anyway. *(Beat.)* I'm so hungry and cold. It's not fair. How come he's in charge and can do whatever he wants? I can't wait to be an adult. That pig ate an entire box of crackers, and we only got to share one. Well, they got to share two. But that's not enough! We're growing boys. We need food. I really could go for some s'mores now. Camping stinks! I wonder if the bears have any food. *(Beat.)* Yeah, right. Like I'm going in that cave to find out. Is it hibernation time? I think it is! So they won't be coming home to eat me! They're already home! And asleep! And I'm talking out loud! And that must be annoying if you're trying to sleep! And I'm so dead! I'm shutting up now! Sorry, bears!

(A troop of Indian chiefs enters.)

GUS: Look, a kid!

FRANK: What are you doing here?

OLIVER: Uh, my troop leader left me out here to die.

FRANK: I don't get you guys with your badges and stuff.

OLIVER: Oh no, it's not for a badge; he just wants me to die.

GUS: How come?

OLIVER: I asked for s'mores.

ZAK: S'mores are excellent! We were just going to have some.

OLIVER: You were?

MR. NICK: Would you like to join us?

OLIVER: Would I! But . . . I guess I have to stay here.

GUS: Why?

OLIVER: My leader said that he'd come back in the morning . . . well, that he *might* come back in the morning to see if the bears ate me—

FRANK: Bears? Are there bears around here?

MR. NICK: Rarely.

GUS: That leader sounds like a jerk.

OLIVER: He is! He ate a whole box of crackers, and we were forced to share only one.

ZAK: So you asked for s'mores.

FRANK: Makes sense.

MR. NICK: That's not right. Who is this man?

OLIVER: Mr. Crumble.

MR. NICK: Well, I'll see about this Mr. Crumble when we get back to town. In the meantime, why don't you have hot dogs and s'mores with us?

ZAK: What's your name anyway?

OLIVER: Oliver.

MR. NICK: Oliver, you are now an honorary Indian Chief.

OLIVER: Thanks, sir!

MR. NICK: And since you're one of us now, you must call me by my real name.

FRANK: Mr. Nick!

MR. NICK: No, no, Frank. Oliver is an Indian Chief. He must call me Nick.

OLIVER: OK, Nick.

MR. NICK: Much better. Now about those s'mores . . . Let's go find ourselves some.

OLIVER: Find them?

MR. NICK: Dodge, why don't you explain what we do to Oliver here.

(DODGE has appeared out of nowhere.)

DODGE: Right, Nick.

(MR. NICK, ZAK, GUS, and FRANK exit.)

DODGE: It's like this, Ollie. We aren't Indian Chiefs at all.

OLIVER: You're not? But—

DODGE: Don't interrupt. **We're not Indian Chiefs. We live by our own rules. Like you, we were discarded as troublemakers, so Nick picked us up and helped us. We're like brothers. Because we don't have anything ourselves, we have to work together. Be our own family. Since we don't have the money for fancy camping trips, we do a little Robin Hood–type stuff. Nothing big. Just enough to have a good time.**

OLIVER: Robin Hood stole from the rich and gave to the poor. How—

DODGE: **You sure do interrupt! Anyway, as I was going to say, we just take a little of this and a little of that from the rich campers so we can get by. For instance, we might take a little chocolate, a few graham crackers, a marshmallow or ten and make some s'mores. Is there anything wrong with that?**

(OLIVER takes a breath to answer.)

DODGE: Don't interrupt! I'll tell you—no! Are we hurting anyone? Don't interrupt! No. It's all good. We're just taking what we need and no more. No harm done. So, are you one of us, Ollie, or do you want to wait around here for the bears to tear you apart? Just like the bears, we have to take what we need to survive. It's a basic animal instinct.

OLIVER: I guess that makes sense. As long as you just take what you need and only from people who have plenty of stuff.

DODGE: So, let's go!

(DODGE and OLIVER exit. MR. CRUMBLE enters.)

MR. CRUMBLE: Oliver? Where are you, you lousy brat! I've had a change of heart since I'm such a kind, good man. You can stay at camp this once so your parents don't sue me. If it were up to me, though, you'd stay here to rot. So let's go! Oliver? Oliver! Where are you, boy?

Scene 2: Taking

MOM: Where's our son?

DAD: Where's Oliver?

MR. CRUMBLE: Um, he wandered off last night. I looked for him all night. I was so worried. But he does have problems following directions. You may want to take him to a learning specialist or a juvenile detention center. Your son has problems, I'm sorry to say.

DAD: Excuse me?

MOM: Our son is a fine young man!

MR. CRUMBLE: Oh, yes. Of course he is. In his own little *(Whispering.)* annoying *(In a normal voice.)* way.

DAD: What did you say?

MR. CRUMBLE: Uh, ahoy ye maties! I was practicing for our boating trip next week.

DAD: Uh-huh. Well, you had better find my son and find him fast!

MOM: Who knows what could have happened to him!

DAD: We're going to look for him. Let's meet back here in an hour. And you'd better have Oliver with you or you will be in big, big trouble, Mr. Crumble!

MR. CRUMBLE: Yes, sir. Of course, sir!

(MOM and DAD exit.)

MR. CRUMBLE: Oliver!

(MR. CRUMBLE exits. DODGE and OLIVER enter.)

OLIVER: Where are we?

DODGE: We're at a camping site for tourists. Look at all the stuff they've got! New tents, mini-heaters, a grill, inflatable mattresses . . . You liked those s'mores last night, right?

OLIVER: I did.

(MR. NICK, ZAK, GUS, and FRANK enter.)

GUS: Jackpot!

ZAK: This place is great!

DODGE: I was just saying to Ollie here that this is his chance to prove he's one of us.

MR. NICK: Very true, Dodge. Oliver, be a good boy and get us a nice breakfast. No one will ever suspect you of being anything but a tourist. It's perfect! You have such an innocent face.

OLIVER: I don't know . . .

ZAK: You knew last night when you were eating our food . . .

OLIVER: Yes, but . . .

FRANK: Are you scared?

OLIVER: No!

GUS: So, what are you waiting for?

MR. NICK: Tell you what. We'll just leave you alone for a bit. We'll wait for you on the outskirts of the camp-site. You either come back with breakfast or we'll lead you back to the bear's cave, and you can see if they're hungry this morning.

OLIVER: What?

DODGE: Old Nick here is just kidding. But don't let us down, Ollie. We're depending on you to do the right thing. You're one of us, and we're a family. We help each other out. Never take more than we need, and never take from people that don't have.

(MR. NICK, DODGE, ZAK, GUS, and FRANK exit.)

OLIVER: Now what? No matter what I do, everything gets messed up. I can't do anything right. I don't want to steal, but if I don't I'll go hungry and I'll have to be alone. I don't think I can survive in the woods on my own. I don't think I can find my way home either. Even if I get out of the woods, then I'll have to get all the way back to my house, and that's a very long way without a car. Am I really greedy and bad? I was hungry. And we were camp-ing. Was it so bad to ask for s'mores? I can't be-lieve Mr. Crumble left me alone to freeze to death! Is it so bad to steal now? You need to eat to sur-vive, right? It's a matter of life and death. The people at this camp seem to be doing well for them-selves. What's the harm? *(Starts looking around.)* This looks just like my mom's sweater. And these are just like my dad's work boots! Weird. Would I steal from my own family? Could this be my family's campsite?

(GUS enters.)

GUS: How ya doin'?

OLIVER: I think maybe this might be my parents' stuff.

GUS: You're kidding, right?

OLIVER: No! This looks like my mom's earrings and that looks like my dad's jacket—

GUS: No way! You are one lucky guy.

OLIVER: What do you mean? I'm the unluckiest guy in the world!

GUS: You're kidding, right? Do you know what this means? If this is your parents' campsite that means that they're here looking for you. No one came looking for me.

OLIVER: They didn't?

GUS: No. I got lost and Mr. Nick found me. I always thought my parents would come, but they didn't. But my parents didn't like me anyway. They fought a lot. Once I heard my dad say that he wished he didn't have kids.

OLIVER: He probably didn't mean it.

GUS: He meant it. I was always doing stupid things. I hated to eat vegetables, and I'm not good at baseball. I broke a trophy of his once. He was really mad at me. Actually, I kinda wanted to be lost. I sort of ran away on purpose. But I thought they'd look for me. I thought they'd be worried and come looking for me. I ran away a couple of times before, but I always went back home. I don't know why I thought this time would be different. I just thought if I didn't come home for long enough, they'd ... I don't know ... care or notice or something. But, they didn't. So. You're lucky. That's all.

OLIVER: So what should I do?

GUS: Maybe you should just stay here.

OLIVER: What about Mr. Nick?

GUS: Oh yeah. Maybe ... Can you just steal something so he won't be mad? Your parents probably wouldn't mind.

OLIVER: I don't know.

(MR. NICK enters quickly.)

MR. NICK: Kid, you're coming with me.

OLIVER: What?

MR. NICK: Your parents are offering a reward for finding you. I'm going to get that reward!

OLIVER: No, I'm staying here.

MR. NICK: If it wasn't for me and my boys, you might have starved or frozen or been eaten by bears!

OLIVER: But my parents are going to come back here anyway!

MR. NICK: Listen, you ungrateful boy, you had better help me get that reward! With that reward the boys and I could get a nice place to live, and we wouldn't have to steal anymore.

OLIVER: Well . . .

(MOM and DAD enter.)

MOM: Oliver! You're here!

DAD: Son? Where have you been?

MOM: Are you OK?

OLIVER: I'm OK. Mr. Crumble kicked me out of the campsite and we were starving, so Mr. Nick here found me and . . . well . . .

MR. NICK: I saved the boy!

DAD: Mr. Nick, we've seen some of your boys. I can't help thinking that their parents are looking for them.

MR. NICK: No, these boys are abandoned!

GUS: Mr. Nick takes care of us!

MOM: Oliver, you're coming home with us now.

MR. NICK: And the reward?

DAD: Mr. Nick, we will give you the reward after you

check that these boys' parents aren't looking for them. Then, and only then, will we give you some money to help care for them.

GUS: He takes good care of us, sir.

MOM: We shall see.

MR. NICK: I'll turn good! You'll see!

DAD: Until then . . .

OLIVER: What about Mr. Crumble?

DAD: Mr. Crumble will be punished. And he will surely lose his job.

MOM: Let's go home.

OLIVER: Good-bye, Gus.

GUS: Good-bye, Oliver.

TALK BACK!

1. This is based on the Charles Dickens story *Oliver Twist*. How is it different? How is it similar?

2. Do you think something like this could truly happen today?

3. Is Dodge a bad person?

4. Have you ever stayed silent while something bad happens to someone else (like the other campers did when Oliver was sent away)? Why does this happen?

5. If you were starving, how far would you go to eat?

6. How can an actor convincingly pretend to be starving?

7. In British slang, what does "nick" mean? Dickens often gave his characters names that described them in some way. If you were a character in a story, what colorful name might you give yourself?

ORPHAN

10F, 1M

WHO

FEMALES	MALES
Aaliyah	Vincent Carter
Amber	
Bailey	
Judy Carter	
Sonya	
Alexis	
Autumn	
Hope	
Shelby	
Sister James	

WHERE Scene 1: In the orphanage; Scene 2: In an abandoned house.

WHEN Present day.

🎭 Try to put yourself in your character's situation. This will help you understand why they act in the way they do and say the things they say.

✎ I watched a documentary where a bunch of girls were left to live alone for a short time. In the documentary, the girls were given food. (In another similar documentary, boys were in the same situation. They were very messy!) However, it got me to thinking—what would it be like if kids had to take care of themselves without adults or any help at all? Write your own play about this situation.

Scene 1: Alone

SONJA: I don't know why they make us do those things. They're humiliating.

ALEXIS: No one ever wants us!

AMBER: I don't think there's anyplace in the world where kids our age are told every day they're too old.

AUTUMN: We're over the hill.

SHELBY: It's pathetic. I hate it.

AALIYAH: It's even worse when they come by and say how cute and sad we are, then turn around and adopt a little baby.

BAILEY: There's that one little moment, isn't there, when you think that maybe, maybe they'll choose to take you with them instead.

ALEXIS: But it never happens!

SHELBY: Isn't this where you're supposed to chime in, Hope, and tell us everything will work out?

AUTUMN: You're not living up to your name.

HOPE: I know. Because I don't know . . . it seems so bleak.

SONJA: We're in big trouble now. If Hope doesn't think it will work out . . .

AMBER: What's going on with you, Hope? I thought you

always wanted to live up to your name, since your parents gave it to you.

HOPE: But my parents are dead. I'm sick of all of this. If my parents really cared about me, they would have stayed alive. I've had hope for years and years, and where did it get me? Nowhere. I'm still alone. We're all still alone. No one adopted us when we were babies, so now we're doomed. No one ever adopts kids as old as us. No one! Who wants an angry, old kid? Not a single person in the universe! If one more person looks at me with sad eyes, then just walks away shaking her head, I'll punch her in the nose! I swear it. I've had enough. I don't feel like being nice and sweet anymore. I've had enough. People aren't supposed to live like this—always waiting for someone to come along and see some good in them. You're supposed to have family in your life. And your family has no choice but to think you're decent. It's their job. Instead, we have to do that job ourselves. And it's too hard. I'm sick of it.

BAILEY: I know. Then people wonder why orphan kids who get taken into a foster home are mean sometimes. I mean, no one's cared about you forever and ever, how are you ever supposed to think that things are going to be any different? And you're already old, you've got your own habits and stuff, and the foster family wants you to be just like their kids or the kids they always wanted. How are you supposed to do that? There's only been you all along, and now you're supposed to know how families act. How are you supposed to know? From TV? I hate TV. Nothing's for real. Everyone is rich and happy. I hate those people. I guess . . . I guess we have to accept this life. I guess this is it for us. We need to turn off any hope of it ever being different. This is it, people! We are going to be in this room for the rest of our lives. Together.

ALEXIS: But that's just it, we're together in this.

AALIYAH: Well, yeah, but it's not what we want. I mean, I like you guys, but we're forced to be together.

SHELBY: So are families! You get born into a family and you have to stick with them, even if you hate them, right?

ALEXIS: Right!

SONJA: So maybe this is where we were born to be after all.

AALIYAH: I hate that idea.

BAILEY: So it's our fate.

HOPE: I can see that. It seems cruel, though.

AUTUMN: OK. I have an idea. So maybe other people are born into terrible families that beat or starve them, right? Well, maybe we're one step above them after all. They have families, but at least we know we'd never hurt each other. Not like that anyway.

HOPE: I'm starting to feel better.

(SISTER JAMES enters with JUDY and VINCENT, an adult couple.)

SISTER JAMES: This is the ward for the older girls.

JUDY: Look at them. Aren't they sweet, Vincent?

VINCENT: They are. Sister, you are doing a lovely job with these girls.

SISTER JAMES: Alexis, come over and say hello to these lovely folks.

(ALEXIS gets up and walks over to JUDY and VINCENT.)

ALEXIS: Hello.

JUDY: Hello, Alexis.

ALEXIS: Hello.

VINCENT: How do you like it here, Alexis?

ALEXIS: It's fine, but I'd like to have a home, sir.

VINCENT: Call me Vincent. And my wife here is Judy.

ALEXIS: Hello. Again.

SISTER JAMES: Alexis can play the piano.

JUDY: You can, Alexis?

ALEXIS: A little.

VINCENT: Well, that's remarkable.

JUDY: Sister James . . .

(JUDY whispers in SISTER JAMES's ear.)

SISTER JAMES: You may go back and play with your friends now, Alexis.

ALEXIS: You're taking a baby, aren't you?

JUDY: Excuse me?

ALEXIS: Everybody takes the babies. Nobody wants us.

VINCENT: Well, I'm sure someone will. You're a very nice girl. Who wouldn't want a nice girl who plays the piano?

ALEXIS: You.

SISTER JAMES: Alexis! Behave.

AALIYAH: We're sick of this, Sister.

HOPE: Why do you have to bring the people in to see us if they don't want us?

SHELBY: It hurts our feelings.

SONJA: We get so sick of not being wanted.

BAILEY: And the look of pity on their faces.

VINCENT: You girls look like you're well cared for.

AUTUMN: It's not the same.

AMBER: It's not a family.

SISTER JAMES: Enough! Mr. and Mrs. Carter, I don't know what's come over these children.

JUDY: Don't apologize. I can see their point of view.

VINCENT: Well, I also see why parents are less likely to take in older children, though! They are more rebellious.

JUDY: Vincent, you can't blame the children.

SISTER JAMES: I assure you this is unusual. Now should we go get your baby?

VINCENT: Let's.

JUDY: Good-bye, girls.

(SISTER JAMES, JUDY, and VINCENT exit.)

SONJA: I hate this!

ALEXIS: Why did she have to call me over?

BAILEY: Then there's that one second where you think, "Maybe. Maybe this time!"

AUTUMN: But it's always the wrong time.

AALIYAH: And you're always the wrong age.

AMBER: It's our fate, girls.

HOPE: But does it have to be?

(SISTER JAMES returns.)

SISTER JAMES: That behavior in front of potential parents is inexcusable. And you know this. When you get older, you children *are* harder and harder to control, just like Mr. Carter said! But this little rebellion will stop. Do you understand me? We feed and shelter you. No one else will take you in, and we work hard to keep you safe and clean and well fed . . . and this is the thanks we get! Inexcusable. You will be punished. You are never, ever to misbehave in front of adopting parents!

ALEXIS: But why did you have me go talk to them?

SISTER JAMES: Because I thought you were a well-behaved little girl.

SONJA: She is!

HOPE: You make her feel like they might adopt her!

SISTER JAMES: What are you talking about?

AMBER: You make us feel like maybe they might take us.

SISTER JAMES: Girls, I hate to tell you this, but we are your family. And no wonder with the way you misbehave. You should be grateful that the sisters let you stay here. Anyone else would have put you out on the street.

ALEXIS: I'm sorry, Sister.

SISTER JAMES: That's better. There will be no more of this. You will clean the entire orphanage from top to bottom tomorrow. And on any other day you misbehave! And you will change all the babies' diapers.

SHELBY: But Sister, those people still adopted the baby, didn't they?

SISTER JAMES: What difference does that make?

SHELBY: So we didn't do anything bad. Everything worked out.

SISTER JAMES: You're talking back again. I can't have that. And those people will not give the orphanage a donation now. Those donations give you a place to rest your heads. Now they see our girls are unruly. Who wants to donate money to help back-talking, misbehaving girls? I'll tell you who. No one. Now shut your mouths and get to bed. I'll have no more of this. Next time, I won't be so kind.

HOPE: We're sorry, Sister.

(SISTER JAMES exits.)

AALIYAH: What are you all apologizing for?

SHELBY: I hate babies! I don't want to change diapers!

HOPE: I just thought I'd smooth things over. So she's not so mad.

AALIYAH: We need to get out of here.

BAILEY: What?

AALIYAH: It's not going to get better here; it's going to get worse.

AUTUMN: We do take care of each other. We could just do it out there, in the world, instead of in here.

SONJA: But how are we going to get food and shelter? You heard Sister James. She said she gets the money to keep us from donations. Where are we going to get donations?

AMBER: We're cleverer than Sister James. We can figure something out.

Scene 2: Together

BAILEY: Who's going to clean this place? It's a dump.

AUTUMN: Why don't you do it?

BAILEY: Because I don't want to. Besides, I got us some bread last night. What did you do?

AUTUMN: Big deal. You stole some bread.

BAILEY: I didn't steal anything.

SONJA: Did you steal it, Bailey?

BAILEY: No! Doesn't anyone listen to me? I said no.

SONJA: How did you get it then?

BAILEY: Well . . .

AUTUMN: She stole it.

BAILEY: I didn't! They threw it out.

SHELBY: We ate bread that was in the garbage? Yuck!

BAILEY: It was good! It was fine. And it wasn't touching anything bad.

SHELBY: You guys, we ate garbage bread!

AMBER: For all we know, that's what the orphanage gave us.

AUTUMN: It was in the garbage, Amber.

AMBER: Did you see anything wrong with it yesterday?

SHELBY: I thought it tasted weird now that I think about it.

AMBER: No, you didn't.

AUTUMN: Yes, she did! And so did I!

BAILEY: Then get your own bread next time!

HOPE: Let's not fight.

AMBER: Too late.

HOPE: Really. It doesn't help. I'll clean the house.

BAILEY: But you always do it. Someone else should.

(AALIYAH and ALEXIS enter.)

AALIYAH: I hate begging!

SONJA: What did you get?

AALIYAH: Five dollars in change. Almost.

SONJA: What can we get for five dollars?

ALEXIS: The police almost took us away.

AALIYAH: People kept asking why we weren't in school, and someone called over a police officer.

HOPE: What did you do?

ALEXIS: We ran.

AALIYAH: That's why we don't have much money.

SONJA: Can we get a pizza for five dollars?

AMBER: No.

AUTUMN: We could share five hamburgers.

SONJA: But there are eight of us!

ALEXIS: I'm so hungry!

HOPE: That doesn't even include anything to drink.

BAILEY: We need more money.

AALIYAH: How? We tried as hard as we could.

SONJA: There must be something.

AUTUMN: We could steal.

SHELBY: Or eat out of the trash—that bread we had yesterday was from the trash!

ALEXIS: Ew!

BAILEY: At least we didn't starve!

HOPE: Don't start that again.

SONJA: We need food now!

AMBER: I have a confession to make.

AALIYAH: You have money!

SONJA: You stole!

AMBER: No, neither of those things. I went to school yesterday.

ALEXIS: What was it like?

AMBER: Well, it didn't go very well. I thought I could just blend in, but first of all, we're a lot dirtier than the other kids. I thought there would be poor kids, too, but not like me. And all the kids kept saying, "Who are you? Where are you from?" I didn't know what to tell them. I thought I could just slip in and no one would notice me. Then I went to a classroom. There was only exactly the right number of desks. There were no extras. And the kids ratted me out. They showed the teacher I was there, then the teacher took me to the principal's office.

SHELBY: You didn't tell them about us?

AMBER: I didn't tell them anything! I mean, I told them a fake address and that my parents came here from Arizona, but I don't think she believed me. She was making a phone call, and I ran away.

ALEXIS: Did she chase you?

AMBER: No. But here's the other part. Behind the school there was a trash can with food in it. A lot of it.

SHELBY: But it was in the trash!

BAILEY: But it's food!

SONJA: I'm hungry.

HOPE: I know no one wants to think this, but maybe we should go back to the orphanage.

AALIYAH: But they didn't treat us right!

HOPE: I know it wasn't great, but at least they fed us and we had a room. When it gets cold here, we're going to freeze!

ALEXIS: But we'll have money by then.

HOPE: How are we ever going to get money?

AUTUMN: We've only been here a little while. We can't figure everything out right away.

HOPE: What if we never figure it out? And Amber found out that we can't go to school. The police chased Alexis and Aaliyah when they tried to beg for money. It doesn't look good. We're talking about eating out of garbage cans! That's not being treated right either. I think maybe the orphanage was better.

SONJA: You're forgetting something.

AUTUMN: What's that?

SONJA: Sister James was mad. They might not take us back.

HOPE: Maybe if we're very, very good and change lots of diapers and clean the entire orphanage from top to bottom for a week, Sister James will take us back.

SHELBY: I hate changing diapers.

AALIYAH: I don't want to be her slave. I want to do whatever I want.

BAILEY: We're living in filth now. Already! And it's only the beginning. It's going to get worse.

AALIYAH: And if we go back, we'll be in filth, too. Other people's filth. We'll be cleaning up for everyone else.

HOPE: Don't you see? We can't survive like this. We're kids. We need people to take care of us. And maybe the Sisters don't do the best job, and they really don't understand us, but at least we were safe. What if someone comes in here? I can't even sleep at night because I'm afraid someone's going to come in here and kill us.

AALIYAH: No one's going to kill us. There's too many of us.

ALEXIS: I've always loved sleeping. Thanks for ruining it for me, Hope. Now I'm scared to sleep, too.

HOPE: I'm not trying to scare anybody. I just think . . . I just think we should go back. We're not safe. What if someone got sick? What would we do?

BAILEY: She might be right.

SHELBY: I don't want to admit it, but . . . she makes sense.

AALIYAH: I'm not going back. No way.

HOPE: **Aaliyah, we just have to go back.**

AALIYAH: I'm not going back! I hated it there. Everyone was mean. And . . . I left Sister James a note.

AUTUMN: What did it say?

AALIYAH: It said that I hated her and I wished she were dead.

ALEXIS: You'll go to hell for that.

AALIYAH: I don't care! I didn't care. I hate her. She was always picking on me.

BAILEY: Thanks a lot! You ruined it for all of us!

SHELBY: We can't jump to conclusions.

HOPE: You could apologize.

AALIYAH: No way!

HOPE: But you could! She's a nun; she's supposed to forgive!

AALIYAH: She won't. And I wouldn't apologize anyway.

ALEXIS: Not even if it means having a home again?

AALIYAH: This is my home.

AUTUMN: Me, too.

SONJA: Not me. I'm hungry!

AMBER: So. Let's have a vote. All those who want to return, raise your hand.
(AMBER, HOPE, SONJA, and BAILEY raise their hands.)

BAILEY: At least until we can figure something better out.

AMBER: All those who want to stay, raise your hands.

(AALIYAH and AUTUMN raise their hands.)

AMBER: Who didn't vote?

(SHELBY and ALEXIS raise their hands.)

ALEXIS: I don't know.

SHELBY: I thought we were a family. We're supposed to do everything together.

BAILEY: Well, I'm going.

HOPE: Me, too.

SONJA: Me, three.

AMBER: Me, four.

ALEXIS: Me, five.

AALIYAH: Alexis, I thought we were going to stick together.

ALEXIS: I can't help it! I'm hungry and . . . it's dirty here.

AALIYAH: Fine! Just go.

SHELBY: Sorry. I'm going, too.

AUTUMN: I thought you hated diapers.

SHELBY: I do.

   (Beat.)

HOPE: Are you sure you won't change your minds?

AALIYAH: Yes.

SONJA: Bye.

ALEXIS: We love you!

SHELBY: Come with us!

AUTUMN: Maybe we should go . . .

AALIYAH: Go then!

AUTUMN: But—

AALIYAH: I don't need anybody.

AUTUMN: Aaliyah . . . Well, I'm going to go. You should
   come, too.

AALIYAH: No, thanks.

AUTUMN: Well . . .

HOPE: You know where we'll be, Aaliyah.

AALIYAH: I hope she lets you in.

AMBER: We hope so, too.

> *(HOPE, AUTUMN, BAILEY, ALEXIS, SONJA, SHELBY, and AMBER exit. AALIYAH is alone.)*

AALIYAH: I'll be fine.

TALK BACK!

1. What do you think will happen to Aaliyah?

2. Will Sister James take the girls back?

3. What would you do if a girl like Amber came to your school?

4. Do you think you'd ever adopt a child when you're older? Would you want a baby or an older kid? Why or why not?

5. If you had to survive on your own, what would you do to get food? Where would you live? Would you go to school?

6. Have you ever thought your life would be more fun without parents? Do you still think so?

7. Can you understand why Sister James, Vincent, and Judy behave as they do?

8. Who is your favorite character and why?

9. Which character is most like you? Which character is least like you? Why?

ATTACK

3F, 3M

WHO

FEMALES   MALES
    Joolz   Landon
    Opal   Nate
    Portia   Nico

WHERE   A school classroom.

WHEN   The near future.

🎭   Try to use "time pressure" in this play. Imagine at all times that you are in danger and you need to find a solution *as soon as possible*. You don't have all day. The time is now!

🖋   Back in 1938, there was a radio broadcast of a story called *War of the Worlds* about Martians coming to earth. People who didn't hear the beginning of the broadcast (when they said it was fake) thought it was really happening and got very scared. Write a play or a story about aliens that would have the same effect.

Scene 1: Confusion

JOOLZ: Come quick!

NICO: What is it?

JOOLZ: Just come in here!

(*LANDON, OPAL, PORTIA, and NATE come on-stage, following JOOLZ and NICO.*)

LANDON: We're supposed to be in geography class.

JOOLZ: Just look!

OPAL: What are we looking at?

JOOLZ: I made this for the science fair.

PORTIA: You brought us in here to look at your science fair project?

JOOLZ: It's meant to show any disturbance near the earth's atmosphere.

NATE: Cool.

OPAL: Why is it going crazy like that? Is it broken?

JOOLZ: That's just it!

NICO: What's just it?

NATE: My science project doesn't work right either.

JOOLZ: No, no! It *does* work right, that's the thing!

LANDON: So what does it mean?

JOOLZ: It means that there's a severe disturbance in the earth's atmosphere.

NICO: So what does that mean, Joolz?

JOOLZ: It means something big is going to happen.

PORTIA: Like what?

JOOLZ: Like an asteroid is about to hit the earth.

NATE: Why wouldn't we hear that on the news?

LANDON: Maybe no one wants us to know.

OPAL: Why not?

PORTIA: This is scaring me. Are we going to die?

JOOLZ: I don't know. But something's going to happen—and soon.

NATE: I still think they'd tell us on the news if something were going to happen.

OPAL: What if they don't know?

NICO: Are you telling me that scientists can't figure out what Joolz figured out with her science project?

PORTIA: It does sound a little silly when you say it like that.

JOOLZ: What do you mean?

LANDON: How could you know more than scientists who have really huge, expensive equipment?

JOOLZ: Why couldn't I? They don't have my machine.

PORTIA: Don't you think they'd have better machines? I mean, they have more money than you. And they went to college and everything.

JOOLZ: Maybe I did something original, something they didn't think about.

NATE: Joolz, you're smart, but I don't think you're as smart as scientists.

JOOLZ: Nobody believes me? You guys, I'm right about this. Something huge is going to happen here! Doesn't anyone believe me?

PORTIA: I'm afraid to believe you, Joolz. If I believe you, it means I have to be afraid for my life. I don't want to do that. If you're right about this, we could all get smushed by an asteroid or something! I'm really young; I don't want to die. So this is way too scary to think about. Couldn't you be wrong?

JOOLZ: Well, maybe.

PORTIA: I'm sorry, Joolz, but I just have to believe that your machine is wrong and that everything's OK. I have to agree with Nate that it would have been on the news if something terrible were about to happen to the earth.

JOOLZ: What if the government didn't want to tell us?

PORTIA: Why would the government want to keep this a secret? Why are you trying to scare us like this? Did it ever occur to you that you could be wrong? I think you're being really cruel, Joolz. If this is a joke, it isn't funny. So just stop it now.

JOOLZ: Portia, I'm not joking. You guys have to believe me. I think something's happening!

NICO: Well, what are we supposed to do then?

OPAL: Should we tell someone?

LANDON: Who would we tell? What would they do?

PORTIA: This isn't happening! It's all a joke. I'm going to geography class.

(PORTIA exits.)

NATE: I gotta side with Portia here. I think it would be on the news if this was really happening, Joolz. Plus, I have to bring up my grade in geography. Last week I failed the test about the state capitals.

(NATE exits.)

OPAL: Seriously, Joolz, should we be doing something or telling someone if this is true?

JOOLZ: I don't know.

NICO: Should we call the news?

LANDON: But what if she's wrong? Then we'll look like jerks.

JOOLZ: Guys, I am more certain about this than I've ever been about anything in my life. I know I've done other experiments that haven't turned out right like the robot to clean my room and the dust eliminator that melted my fish tank, but this one is good. This machine is right. I know it! I just know it. I am certain there is something going on, a big disturbance at the earth's atmosphere. It's possible that nothing at all will happen, but I doubt it. This response is too strong. Right now, something is entering the earth. I don't know what—or who—but I know it's big and it's coming and there's no stopping it. I don't think there's anywhere we can run or hide. I think we just need to brace ourselves for the worst—

LANDON: What's the worst?

JOOLZ: The total destruction of life on earth or . . .

OPAL: Or what?

JOOLZ: . . . or a takeover of our planet.

LANDON: What do you mean?

NICO: Are you saying you think aliens are going to take over the earth? Because that's crazy.

JOOLZ: I know it sounds crazy, Nico, but it's possible. How could we be the only living creatures in the universe? Isn't it possible for there to be other forms of life that are more advanced than we are?

OPAL: I didn't think anything was more advanced than people.

JOOLZ: We don't know of anything, but that doesn't mean that nothing else exists.

LANDON: If there are creatures smarter than us, how come we've never seen them before?

JOOLZ: Maybe they never bothered with us before.

NICO: That's crazy.

OPAL: It is sort of stupid to think that we're the only forms of life in the universe. The universe is huge, right? It only makes sense that there are other things out there.

NICO: If those things are so smart, why would they want to come here? If their planet is so terrific, what do they want with us?

LANDON: Maybe they need to eat humans to live.

JOOLZ: Don't be silly, Landon. This is serious.

LANDON: I was being serious! We don't know.

OPAL: I'm scared.

NICO: Do you think they'll be green or bumpy or what?

OPAL: We can't know, can we?

LANDON: I always think it's strange that aliens on TV might be different colors and have strange faces, but they always have two legs and breathe the same atmosphere we do. How come they're not more different? Plus, they speak English. I mean, even the French don't speak English. Why would aliens?

JOOLZ: Be serious, Landon.

LANDON: I am being serious! I want to know.

OPAL: Well, you just might find out if Joolz is right.

JOOLZ: If I'm right, something is going to happen any second now. Look at my machine!

NICO: It's really going nuts now!

(The lights flicker.)

JOOLZ: Here we go . . .

OPAL: Joolz, I'm sorry to say this, but I really hope you're wrong about this.

JOOLZ: Opal, I'm sorry to say this, but I'm absolutely sure I'm right . . .

Scene 2: Chaos

OPAL: Do you hear that?

LANDON: Hear what?

OPAL: In your head.

LANDON: I don't hear anything in my head.

NICO: As usual.

LANDON: Shut up.

OPAL: Shhh! We need to keep quiet and calm.

JOOLZ: Good idea.

OPAL: That's what I hear in my head, except I don't think it's me thinking it.

JOOLZ: I feel weird.

NICO: What is it?

(PORTIA enters suddenly.)

PORTIA: What did you do, Joolz? Something weird is going on. I don't like this at all.

JOOLZ: I didn't do anything. I just reported what I knew. Oh, my head!

PORTIA: What's happening?

OPAL: Do you hear anything, Portia?

PORTIA: No. I'm just . . . I know something's happening.

JOOLZ: I feel like . . . I think . . . something's trying to read my mind. Or . . . something's trying to suck information out of my head. It hurts.

(NATE enters.)

NATE: Joolz, come with me.

JOOLZ: Where?

NATE: Come with me.

LANDON: Just Joolz?

NATE: Just Joolz.

NICO: Why?

NATE: She just needs to come with me, OK?

OPAL: How come, Nate?

NATE: Come with me, Joolz. Now.

JOOLZ: You need to tell me why.

NATE: I can't tell you why.

NICO: How come?

NATE: I only know what I'm told.

PORTIA: What you're told?

NATE: Joolz needs to come with me now. That's all I know.

OPAL: Who's telling you this?

NATE: They're telling me this.

LANDON: Who're they?

NATE: I don't know who they are. I just hear my orders. "Bring us Joolz." And I can't disobey. Even if I try. When I try to think of something else, it's like it gets overrun by this other voice. "Bring us Joolz." It just runs through my head constantly. Come with me, Joolz. Please. Everyone, Joolz needs to come with me. Please help me. I want to stop thinking this. I can't even remember my name. "Bring us Joolz. Bring us Joolz." It's like a record that plays over and over. We need to go to the playground. Now. Joolz, do as I say. It's important. Don't ask me why. I don't know why. I'm not allowed to tell you anymore. I just know you need to come with me. It's a matter of life or death.

PORTIA: Whose life or death?

NATE: Everyone's life or death. Please, Joolz. This voice is driving me crazy. It just won't stop. Joolz, if you don't come with me, it will all be over for everyone here. I'm sorry if this is wrong, but I will do whatever I need to do to get this voice to stop. There's no time left. Come with me, Joolz.

JOOLZ: No.

PORTIA: You have to go! We could all be killed!

JOOLZ: Why would everyone be killed? It doesn't make any sense.

OPAL: Maybe they don't care about human life. Or the life of anything else on earth for that matter.

JOOLZ: I doubt that.

LANDON: Why?

JOOLZ: I don't know. I just doubt that. There must be something they want, and if they kill everyone and everything, they won't get it.

NICO: Maybe it's all just a game to them.

PORTIA: *(Shouting.)* She's coming!

OPAL: *(Shouting.)* No, she's not!

PORTIA: What?

OPAL: We can't let them take Joolz! That would be wrong! She's our friend. We can't let her be killed.

NICO: We don't know that they'd kill her.

LANDON: We don't know that they won't.

JOOLZ: My head hurts so much!

NATE: So does mine!

OPAL: I don't think they're good.

NICO: Maybe they just want the machine. We could bring them the machine.

PORTIA: Who's going to bring them the machine? I'm not.

NATE: They don't want the machine. They want Joolz.

JOOLZ: I'm not coming. They need to say what they want.

NATE: I told you, they want you.

PORTIA: They could kill our mothers and our fathers— everyone we know and love. Joolz, you have to go. You have to save us all.

JOOLZ: I just don't believe it.

PORTIA: You're being selfish!

OPAL: I have to admit I'm torn. I don't know what to do. Joolz, I don't think it's fair for them to take you, but I also don't think it's fair that everyone has to die because you won't go.

LANDON: We don't know what they want. It could be no big deal, anyway.

NICO: They said it was life or death, though.

LANDON: Maybe it's their life or death, not ours. Maybe there's something about Joolz, maybe even something she's wearing, that they want.

OPAL: If that was the case, there ought to be dozens of

other kids they could find. She buys her clothes in a store like the rest of us. Her stuff isn't one of a kind.

PORTIA: Let's face it. They want her scientific knowledge. Whatever she's made here—it's for real. She knows something. She has some kind of important information. That's what they want. Why shouldn't she give it to them? It might be perfectly reasonable.

OPAL: But we don't know that.

LANDON: Maybe they want her to be their bride. Maybe they want her to have an alien baby.

JOOLZ: Gross! I'm definitely not going!

PORTIA: You say you're interested in science. Well, this is an experiment, Joolz! Your greatest experiment yet. You could discover something about alien life forms. About how they think. About what they know. About how they live. Think about it! Think how important that could be!

JOOLZ: You don't care about me or science. You just want me to leave. You just want to live.

PORTIA: Of course I just want to live! We all do! I can't believe how selfish you are!

NATE: It's time. You need to come now, Joolz. You need to come now.

NICO: Joolz, you need to make a decision. I know this is scary. We don't know what they want exactly. We don't know what they're like—if they're good or bad. But we do know that possibly the fate of humankind is in your hands. They want you. They've threatened us if you don't go with them. It could mean the end of our lives. Maybe they don't mean it. Maybe it's a bluff. But what if it's not, Joolz? What if they mean it? What if they really do mean to kill the rest of us if you don't go out to meet them? And . . . maybe they'll kill you anyway. Maybe this is your only chance to live. I don't really know what I'd do in your situation. I know we're asking a lot. But—I think you have to go. It's the right thing to do. If you don't, I guess I'll understand, but . . . Joolz, for the sake of all of us, do what they say. Go with Nate.

PORTIA: If you don't go, I'll push you out.

OPAL: Portia!

PORTIA: I am not going to die!

OPAL: Listen to us! Why are we so willing to sacrifice our friend? It isn't right!

LANDON: It could be our only chance!

NATE: Come with me now, Joolz! There's not much time left!

PORTIA: Landon, help me push her out of here.

JOOLZ: No! I don't think they mean it!

NICO: You think this is some kind of game?

LANDON: It's a lot of trouble for a game.

JOOLZ: I think it's a test.

OPAL: You can't know that.

JOOLZ: I think I do know that.

PORTIA: How?

JOOLZ: I just do.

PORTIA: Help me, Landon.

(PORTIA tries to pull JOOLZ out of the room. NATE joins her. After a moment, LANDON joins as well.)

JOOLZ: No!

(OPAL pulls JOOLZ in the other direction to keep her in the room. NICO pulls OPAL out of the way and gives JOOLZ a final push offstage.)

OPAL: No!

(Beat. NICO reenters.)

OPAL: How could you?

NICO: I just couldn't take the chance.

OPAL: How could you! We don't know what they'll do with her.

NICO: We'll find out soon.

TALK BACK!

1. Would you believe Joolz in Scene 1? Why or why not?

2. Would you want Joolz to go or stay? Explain your reasoning.

3. What do you think the aliens wanted?

4. Are Portia, Nate, Landon, and Nico smart or traitors when they push Joolz outside? Why?

5. Do you think there are aliens out there? Does this idea scare or interest you?

6. Would you want to have contact with life from another planet? What would you want to ask an alien?

7. In ancient times, before we knew much about science, people thought gods controlled all the things they couldn't explain like rain and thunder. Nowadays people sometimes think ghosts and aliens exist to explain things they don't understand, like bright lights in the sky and objects moving on their own. Do you think someday everything will be explained by science, or do you think there are ghosts and aliens on earth today?

TWO SISTERS
(AND A BROTHER)

2F, 1M

WHO

FEMALES   MALES
   Darla   Jack
   Erin

WHERE The Sharps's living room.

WHEN Present day.

🎭 Make decisions about the lives of the characters in this story before the play starts. How old are they? Where do they live? What are their parents like?

✍ I confess, I'm Erin in this story. This is how I felt when I was a kid. Write a play from Darla's or Jack's viewpoint.

Scene 1: Two Sisters

(ERIN is doing her homework.)

DARLA: You just don't dance as well as I do.

ERIN: Sure I do.

DARLA: No, you don't. People laugh at you when you're not looking.

ERIN: How do you know?

DARLA: I've seen them.

ERIN: No, you haven't.

DARLA: Sure, I have.

ERIN: Why are they laughing then?

DARLA: Because you're chubby.

ERIN: No, I'm not.

DARLA: Yes, you are. No one tells you that because they feel sorry for you.

ERIN: You don't know anything.

DARLA: I know everything. I'm smarter than you.

ERIN: No, you're not. I get better grades than you.

DARLA: That's because the teachers are jealous of me.

ERIN: The teachers are not jealous. That doesn't even make sense.

DARLA: I'm just stating the facts.

ERIN: You don't know what facts are.

DARLA: I know better than you do. I'm older and I know more. It's a fact.

ERIN: You're stupid and no one likes you.

DARLA: Everybody likes me. Mom and Dad like me best.

ERIN: You wish.

DARLA: I don't need to wish; I know.

ERIN: You don't know anything. You're a creep.

DARLA: You're jealous.

ERIN: How could I be jealous of you? I don't even like you.

DARLA: I'm smarter and I dance better and I'm not chubby and I'm older and Mom and Dad like me best.

ERIN: You're a big, fat liar. That's what you are.

DARLA: *(Yelling.)* Dad, Erin called me a fat liar! *(Beat.)* See? He told you to "watch it"!

ERIN: You're the one who started this.

DARLA: And I'm the one to finish it.

ERIN: So get lost so I can do my homework.

DARLA: I'm done my homework.

ERIN: I bet you did it wrong.

DARLA: Mom checked it.

ERIN: Mom doesn't have to check my homework because I do it right.

DARLA: Mom checks mine because she likes me better.

ERIN: Mom said that you were a pain in the neck.

DARLA: No, she didn't.

ERIN: Wanna bet?

DARLA: You don't have any money.

ERIN: I do. I save my money. You're the one with no money.

DARLA: That is so boring. Saving your money. You always do really boring things.

ERIN: At least I have friends.

DARLA: I have friends.

ERIN: Who?

DARLA: Tessa.

ERIN: Tessa is your friend because Mom and Dad invite her and she's too polite to say no.

DARLA: At least my friends aren't little babies like you.

ERIN: I'm not a baby.

DARLA: You're a tiny baby. You probably still wet yourself.

ERIN: I'm way too old for that and you know it.

DARLA: You cry and wet yourself like a baby.

ERIN: You wish.

DARLA: I know. And I'm going to tell everyone.

ERIN: You wouldn't.

DARLA: I would.

ERIN: Who would you tell?

DARLA: Everyone.

ERIN: No one would believe you. I'm smarter than you. Everyone knows that.

DARLA: No, they don't, fatty.

ERIN: Don't call me fatty. I'm not fat, chicken legs.

DARLA: *(Yelling.)* Dad, Erin called me chicken legs! *(Beat.)* You're in trouble now. Dad likes me best.

ERIN: Why did you do that? You say things to me all the time, and you make me say bad things about you. I was just sitting here doing my homework, and you came up to me and started saying mean things. And the minute I say something back to you, because you won't stop, I get in trouble. It's not fair. You're trying to make Dad turn against me. You want him to like you best. So you lie. You're horrible. I hate you.

DARLA: *(Yelling.)* Dad, Erin said she hates me!

ERIN: *(Yelling.)* I didn't say anything to her, Dad! I'm just trying to do my homework! *(Beat.)* Dad says I'm supposed to just do my homework and not speak to you, so go away now. I don't want to see or hear you anymore. You drive me crazy. And you're mean.

DARLA: I can't help that you're a baby.

ERIN: *I'm* a baby, Darla? You're the one who cries to Daddy whenever I say anything even a little bit mean back to you. You could say sixty things to me, and I don't say anything. If I say even one thing back, you cry to Dad. Who's the baby? I think it's you.

DARLA: *(Yelling.)* Dad? Daddy! Erin called me a baby! *(Beat.)* You're in trouble.

ERIN: Because of you.

DARLA: You'd better hurry up and go get punished.

ERIN: You'd better leave me alone when I get back.

(ERIN exits.)

DARLA: "Look at me! I'm Erin. I'm perfect. And I'm a fat little fatty. I think I can dance. I think I'm good at school and people think I'm funny." People think you're funny *looking*, stupid. She thinks she's better than me, but she's not. *(Louder.)* You're not, Erin! Dad likes me best. *(Normal volume.)* Dad's going to punish her. *(Beat.)* I think I'll do Erin's homework—wrong. That will be fun. I have to do something to pass the time. Look at this baby stuff. Anybody can do this. There's no way she's going to manage things in my grade. She's going to fail and have to work at the gas station. She's going to be the only girl working at the gas station. And she'll smell like gas and be dirty all the time. Serves her right for being so mean to me. I do so have friends. I have lots of friends. *(Yelling.)* She said I didn't have friends, Dad! That hurt my feelings. Tell her to leave me alone, Daddy! *(Quietly.)* Stupid Erin.

(ERIN returns.)

ERIN: Dad says to do your homework.

DARLA: I did my homework.

ERIN: I'm not supposed to talk to you, and you're not supposed to talk to me.

DARLA: You're talking to me now.

ERIN: Not anymore. I'm done.

(ERIN sits down and looks back at her homework.)

ERIN: You drew on my homework!

DARLA: No, I didn't.

ERIN: Yes, you did.

DARLA: You're talking to me.

ERIN: Fine.

(ERIN starts erasing.)

ERIN: You drew right over my answers. I have to do them over. Idiot.

DARLA: I'm telling Dad you said that.

ERIN: Go ahead. Just leave me alone, idiot.

DARLA: I'm telling Dad you said that.

ERIN: I'm just saying the same thing over, idiot.

DARLA: I'm telling Dad you're saying that.

ERIN: OK, idiot. Good-bye.

DARLA: You're the idiot.

ERIN: Dad said not to talk to me.

DARLA: Dad said not to talk to me!

(Beat. ERIN is silent and goes back to doing her homework. DARLA pokes her. ERIN ignores her. DARLA pokes ERIN again. ERIN ignores her. DARLA pokes ERIN again. ERIN swats DARLA's hand away.)

DARLA: Daaad? Erin hit me!

Scene 2: (And a Brother)

(DARLA and ERIN are sitting on opposite sides of the room. ERIN is doing her homework; DARLA is brushing her hair and kicking the chair she's sitting in. JACK enters.)

JACK: What's going on?

(ERIN ignores him. Beat.)

DARLA: Erin was being mean so Dad says we can't talk to each other.

JACK: As usual.

DARLA: What do you mean "as usual"?

JACK: Don't you do this every day?

ERIN: I don't do anything.

DARLA: Yeah, right. You told me Jack kicked you the other day.

ERIN: He did kick me.

JACK: I said I was sorry.

ERIN: I know. It's OK. I mean, it's not OK, but it's over.

JACK: Right.

DARLA: Jack, look at what I can do!

(DARLA does a quick dance move.)

DARLA: My teacher said I was the best.

ERIN: No, she didn't.

DARLA: Yes, she did.

JACK: Don't start again.

ERIN: I'm not starting anything. I'm trying to do my homework.

DARLA: You're *still* not done?

ERIN: If you'd be quiet.

JACK: Don't start again.

ERIN: I'm not starting anything!

(ERIN picks up her books.)

ERIN: Fine! I guess I'll go somewhere else.

DARLA: Good!

(ERIN exits.)

DARLA: Isn't she mean? She shouldn't get to talk to us like that. Like she's the boss or something. Don't you think?

JACK: I don't know.

DARLA: She talks to you like you're stupid. She talks to everybody like that.

JACK: I guess sometimes.

DARLA: I guess all the time! It's our house, too. We should be able to talk here if we want. The world doesn't revolve around her. *(Beat.)* I bet you didn't kick her hard at all the other day. You probably should have kicked her harder.

JACK: Sometimes I'm stronger than I think I am. It was an accident.

DARLA: And she won't stop talking about it. She was going on and on about it. Complaining how you didn't get in trouble and how it really, really hurt. She's such a baby.

JACK: She did get mad. And I really didn't mean it. It was an accident.

DARLA: She's such a baby, I swear.

JACK: You shouldn't swear.

DARLA: Yeah, but she's making me do it.

JACK: She's not making you do it.

DARLA: Sure she is. **She makes me so mad. She thinks she's perfect. Isn't she stuck up sometimes?**

JACK: Yeah.

DARLA: **She bosses everyone around. When Mom and Dad aren't around, she thinks she's the boss. She thinks she can tell everyone what to do. She acts like your mother.**

JACK: I know. She gets suffocating sometimes. She's always trying to take care of me. I can take care of myself.

DARLA: I know! She thinks she's the boss of us.

JACK: I guess she's trying to be nice.

DARLA: No, she's not. She doesn't care about anyone but herself. She's just trying to boss us around and get us to do whatever she wants. I'm not ever going to do anything she wants. I'm the oldest. I should say what everybody does. Everyone should do what I say. I know the most.

JACK: Well, I don't know about that.

DARLA: I do! I know the most. Because I'm the oldest. That's just how it works. So when Mom and Dad aren't here, I'm in charge.

JACK: Why should anyone be in charge? Maybe we should be in charge of ourselves.

DARLA: That's too bad if you don't like it. I'm in charge. You can even ask Dad. You can't fight it. That's the way the world works. The oldest person is in charge. So you and Erin should get used to it.

JACK: Whatever.

DARLA: So do you hate Erin like I do?

JACK: No.

DARLA: Not ever?

JACK: I guess sometimes.

DARLA: I hate her most of the time. She's fat and mean and she can't boss me around.

JACK: She's not fat.

DARLA: Close enough. She looks like a whale in ballet class.

JACK: That's mean. And impossible.

DARLA: She deserves it.

JACK: No, she doesn't.

DARLA: Fine! Take her side. See if I care!

(DARLA exits.)

JACK: Girls are so weird.

(ERIN enters.)

ERIN: Is the coast clear?

JACK: Yeah.

ERIN: Thank God.

JACK: Yeah.

ERIN: She's crying to Dad again. Why does he always listen to her and take her side?

JACK: I don't know.

ERIN: She drives me crazy. I wish she'd just shut her mouth for once. *(Beat.)* I just don't understand why Dad believes her! She calls me names until I can't stand it anymore, then I say something back or hit her, and *she* cries and runs to Daddy! It's not fair. She's an idiot.

JACK: I guess.

ERIN: Am I wrong, Jack?

JACK: No.

ERIN: She just drives me crazy. You know?

JACK: Just leave me out of it, OK? You two are always fighting and putting me in the middle. I don't want to be in the middle. I don't care. I think you're bossy, and she's obnoxious, OK? Is that what you want to hear? I don't know what you want from me. I don't know what to say to you two. I can't agree with you, and I can't not agree. I can't answer you when you say bad things about each other, and I can't not answer you. You're both my sisters. Why do I need to pick sides? And if I say something bad about one of you—Well, I never know when what I say will come back to hurt me. On those rare occasions you actually get along, you gang up on me. It's all just really sick. Why can't you just act normal? Just leave me out of it, OK?

ERIN: Sorry. I didn't mean to put you in the middle of it. I just feel like I sometimes need to get things off my chest and if I tell Mom and Dad . . . then it seems like I'm complaining and it turns into this whole big thing and I get into trouble. I just wanted to talk to someone.

JACK: I know. But you know what I mean, right?

ERIN: Yeah. Sorry. I'll . . . I'll try not to do it. I'll just not talk to anyone.

JACK: That's not what I mean. It's just that I don't know what to say. I don't want to take sides.

ERIN: I know, I know. I'm sorry.

(DARLA enters.)

DARLA: You're talking about me.

ERIN: I'm doing my homework.

JACK: I'm going to watch TV.

DARLA: You're *still* doing your homework?

JACK: Let's watch TV.

DARLA: OK. It's better than watching her do her baby homework.

(JACK and DARLA exit. ERIN sighs and goes back to doing her homework.)

TALK BACK!

1. Do you have brothers and/or sisters? If so, how do you feel about them? If not, do you wish you had brothers or sisters? Why or why not?

2. Which character are you most like? Which character are you least like? Why?

3. Can you understand how all the characters feel?

4. Who's right? Who's wrong? Why?

5. What else could Erin do to get Darla to leave her alone?

6. We know Darla is the oldest. Who's the middle child and who's the youngest?

7. Have you ever felt like you can't win no matter what you do? Give an example of when this happened to you and how it made you feel.

8. If you had a problem whom would you talk to and why?

PUNKED

5F, 4M

WHO

FEMALES
- Astrid
- Carrie
- Clea
- Paisley
- Rogue

MALES
- Angus
- Clayton
- Felix
- Lance

WHERE School.

WHEN Present day.

🎭 Know who your friends are among the characters. Who's your best friend? Who don't you like very much? Be very clear about how you feel about each person onstage.

🖎 Write a play where a problem isn't resolved and see if you can create discussion over what happens in the end!

Scene 1: New Kid

CLAYTON: Have you seen the new kid?

CARRIE: He looks weird.

FELIX: You're telling me. Have you seen that hair?

ASTRID: I'm scared of him.

PAISLEY: People just aren't supposed to look like that.

LANCE: I heard he's crazy.

CLAYTON: He got kicked out of another school.

ASTRID: He did?

FELIX: What for?

LANCE: Probably because he's crazy.

CLAYTON: And I bet he gets in lots of fights.

CARRIE: I've just never seen a kid look like that.

PAISLEY: I never thought people actually dressed like that except on TV.

ASTRID: I wonder what his parents are like. Maybe they're just like him.

FELIX: No way. They probably hate him.

CARRIE: If he's like this now, just imagine what he'll be like when he's older.

ASTRID: Do you think he's mean?

LANCE: Definitely. I bet he gets into fights all the time. I bet that's why he got kicked out of his old school.

CLAYTON: Quiet! He's coming this way.

PAISLEY: What do we say if he talks to us?

FELIX: I'm not scared of him.

ASTRID: I bet you are.

FELIX: I'm not!

(ANGUS enters. He's got spiky hair and is wearing all black.)

ANGUS: Hi.

(ASTRID screams.)

ANGUS: Are you OK?

(ASTRID runs offstage, panicked.)

ANGUS: What's wrong with her?

PAISLEY: She, uh . . . She, uh . . . had to go to the bathroom.

ANGUS: Does she scream every time she has to go?

PAISLEY: Um, yeah. We all do. *(Weakly.)* Aaah. See? I, uh, have to go, too. So . . . bye.

(PAISLEY walks a big circle around ANGUS and exits.)

ANGUS: You guys are a little strange around here.

LANCE: We're strange?

ANGUS: Well, yeah. I've been to lots of places, and I've never seen people scream before they go to the bathroom.

LANCE: So we're strange.

ANGUS: That's what I said. I'm just saying it's an odd thing to do.

LANCE: So we're strange.

ANGUS: Why do you keep saying that?

CLAYTON: Did you ever think maybe *you're* strange?

ANGUS: Sure.

CLAYTON: Oh.

LANCE: 'Cause you are.

ANGUS: So are you.

LANCE: What?

CARRIE: Please don't fight!

ANGUS: Fight? I don't want to fight. I'm just saying we're all strange some of the time.

FELIX: You think everyone is strange?

ANGUS: Let's get on another word. I'm sick of strange.

LANCE: What's wrong with strange?

CLAYTON: Yeah, what's wrong with strange?

ANGUS: We've said it, like, thirty times. Let's say unusual instead.

LANCE: Let's say we don't.

ANGUS: What's your problem?

CARRIE: Please don't fight!

ANGUS: I'm so confused.

FELIX: Listen, we don't want any problems here. We know what happened at your other school.

ANGUS: You do?

FELIX: Well, he heard stuff.

ANGUS: This is a little embarrassing.

CLAYTON: Embarrassing?

ANGUS: Yeah. I mean, I didn't know that you knew. I didn't want people to know.

LANCE: Too late for that.

(PAISLEY and CARRIE enter very slowly and cautiously.

Trying to be invisible, they walk a huge circle around ANGUS, grab their book bags, and exit in a hurry.)

ANGUS: Seriously, what's with those two? Is it because of what they heard about me?

CARRIE: Well, yeah! People hear things and . . . you know. It's natural that they'd be like that. You're just different from the rest of us.

ANGUS: I'm not so different. I think you'll find I'm just like you, really.

LANCE: I doubt that. You're not like us. And we're not like you. We'll never get along. We don't want to get along. I think you'll find there's no one at this school like you. So I hope you like being alone because that's how it's going to be.

ANGUS: That's harsh.

LANCE: Maybe it is harsh. But that's the truth. We're *normal* people here. We're not strange or unusual. We're *normal;* get it? And you're weird. I don't know where you come from or why you came here, but you should get your parents to bring you somewhere else. You don't fit in here. So you should stop harassing people and just get lost. You don't belong here.

ANGUS: Why not?

LANCE: Look at you! You're dressed crazy and your hair is messed up; you're a freak! What about this don't you understand?

FELIX: Calm down, Lance.

LANCE: I don't want to calm down! I want this punk to get out of my face now. I don't want any trouble here.

ANGUS: You're the one starting a fight, not me.

LANCE: You want to fight? OK. Let's fight!

ANGUS: I don't want to fight.

LANCE: Are you scared?

ANGUS: No, I just think it's stupid.

LANCE: Are you calling me stupid?

CARRIE: Please don't fight! I mean it! You're scaring me.

LANCE: He just called me stupid.

ANGUS: No, I said fighting is stupid.

LANCE: So who's stupid now, stupid?

ANGUS: What?

CLAYTON: Even I'm lost now.

LANCE: You like fighting so I guess that makes you stupid.

ANGUS: I don't like fighting.

FELIX: But that's why you were kicked out of your last school.

ANGUS: I wasn't kicked out of my last school. That's what you thought? Oooh. I see. No. I left my last school on purpose. It had nothing to do with fighting. I mean, I've been in a fight before, but it's not like I enjoy it.

CARRIE: So why did you leave your last school then?

ANGUS: **You really don't know anything about me?**

FELIX: Not really, I guess. I mean, we thought . . .

CLAYTON: We heard stuff.

ANGUS: **Weird. Anyway, it's probably better that you don't know about me. I like to be mysterious. Or at least just a regular kid.**

CLAYTON: You're not a regular kid?

LANCE: Look at him. How could he be?

CARRIE: Maybe you should clear up the rumors about you. It might be better.

ANGUS: **OK. I'd rather not tell you, but . . . OK. I'm an animator. I'm sort of famous. I do the cartoon *Harvey Wallbanger*. So it got sort of bad at my old school. People were always bugging me to draw them a picture or give them an autograph and other kids got jealous . . . It was just a bad scene. I hope it's not like that here. No one would leave me alone. I just want a fresh start. So my parents brought me out here. I like it. It's quiet. I can get a lot of** work done at night after my homework. I have guys in Japan who help with the animation now, so that helps. I thought everyone would be really friendly. I hope I'm not wrong. I just want to have a nice, quiet life. And I want to be as normal as possible. I don't want to fight or anything. I just want to be left alone, really. Not that I don't want friends. I just don't want to be hassled. OK? Truce?

FELIX: I love *Harvey Wallbanger*! It's my absolute favorite cartoon. I cannot believe this.

CLAYTON: I like it more than you. And I liked it first.

CARRIE: I know what you said, but do you think maybe . . . could I get your autograph? Oh my God, it's so amazing that you're here!

ANGUS: I really just want to be a regular kid.

CARRIE: Please, just this once? I'll never ask again.

CLAYTON: Yeah, couldn't you make an exception just this once?

ANGUS: I really don't want word about this getting around school. Can you keep a secret?

FELIX: I am excellent at keeping secrets.

LANCE: So you're famous.

ANGUS: I guess. A little.

LANCE: Huh. I wasn't expecting that.

Scene 2: The Old Pattern

ASTRID: Hi, Angus!

ANGUS: *(Drawing.)* Hi.

ASTRID: How ya doing?

ANGUS: Fine.

ASTRID: Whatcha doing?

ANGUS: Working.

ASTRID: Why?

ANGUS: Because I need to. Sorry, Astrid, but do you mind . . . ?

ASTRID: Oh. OK. So I guess I'll see you later?

ANGUS: I guess so.

ASTRID: I hope so.

ANGUS: OK.

ASTRID: OK.

ANGUS: Bye.

ASTRID: Bye, Angus!

    (ASTRID keeps standing there.)

ANGUS: Bye.

ASTRID: Bye!

(ASTRID *finally exits. ROGUE enters. She's also dressed a little bit differently than the others: a long skirt, a ski cap, and a long sweater.*)

ROGUE: Wussup?

ANGUS: Nothing. Just trying to work and no one will leave me alone.

ROGUE: What are you working on?

ANGUS: I don't know. I'm trying to come up with a new character, but it's not working.

ROGUE: Want me to look at it?

ANGUS: Nah. Maybe I just need a break.

ROGUE: OK. Want to do something?

ANGUS: I'm afraid to go anywhere. I keep getting mobbed.

ROGUE: **That's the price of being famous, I guess.**

ANGUS: It's a curse.

ROGUE: Hey, you picked it.

ANGUS: Sort of. It also sort of picked me.

ROGUE: **Come on. You ask for all the attention. You pretend like you don't notice that you dress differently than everyone else, but you have to know** that. This makes you stick out in case that's escaped your attention. It makes you less than invisible. If you didn't want to be looked at you could wear jeans and a T-shirt with a sports logo on it and sneakers. If you didn't want to be noticed, there are definitely things you could do. But the fact is, you like it. Maybe not all the time, every day, but you like it. You act all aggravated when people approach you, but come on. You're talking to me here. There's a part of you that loves being adored. You know, it kills me how people are always buying you stuff—lunch, presents . . . No one gives me anything. And I could use stuff! I'm not rich like you. How come rich people get bought stuff and poor people don't? It's not fair. I wouldn't mind being famous for a day. Or at least during lunch.

ANGUS: I'll buy you a Coke.

ROGUE: You'll buy me two.

ANGUS: Don't be greedy.

(CLEA enters.)

CLEA: Hey, you know it's not nice to tell someone to go away 'cause you're working and then talk to another person even though that other person is doing exactly what that first person was doing, only you're not asking *her* to go away. It's not nice.

ANGUS: What?

CLEA: You told Astrid to leave you alone and now you're talking to *her.*

ANGUS: So?

CLEA: So, that's very rude. In case you didn't know Astrid actually likes you, so you shouldn't be mean to her. Plus, she's a lot cuter than *her* so it doesn't make sense that you'd talk to *her* and not to Astrid. So. You should apologize.

ANGUS: Still not following.

CLEA: Hello? I am speaking English here! Boys are so dense, I swear! You should be talking to Astrid and not her because you are clearly not really working and you hurt her feelings because you said you were, but you aren't because you're talking to her! Don't you see the unfairness, cruelty, and rudeness here? This is obvious. I can't believe you don't see this. Maybe you aren't as cool as you think. But Astrid likes you, so you should be nice. So what are you going to do?

ANGUS: Nothing.

ROGUE: I think you should go away.

CLEA: I think you should mind your own business.

ROGUE: *(Standing.)* I think you should go away.

CLEA: Well . . . I'm just saying . . . It's rude. OK?

(ROGUE steps closer to CLEA. CLEA runs away.)

ANGUS: What was that?

ROGUE: I don't know. Looks like you have a girlfriend.

ANGUS: Astrid? I don't think so. Is there anyone in school more different from me?

ROGUE: I know. And she thinks she's cute, too. Ugh. If anyone called me cute, I'd puke on them.

(FELIX enters.)

FELIX: Hi, Angus? Hi!

ANGUS: Hi, Felix.

FELIX: So I just wanted to say sorry for Clea coming over here. I told her and Astrid that they shouldn't bother you.

ANGUS: Thanks.

FELIX: Yeah. So. *(Beat.)* So. What are you doing?

ANGUS: Nothing. Thinking.

FELIX: Can I help? I mean, I'm just really interested in animation and all. Maybe I might have some ideas.

ANGUS: That's OK.

FELIX: Oh. Are you sure?

ANGUS: Yeah. I'll figure it out. Thanks.

FELIX: Oh. OK. *(Beat.)* OK.

(FELIX starts to exit. LANCE and CLAYTON enter.)

LANCE: So, Angus, Clayton and I were just watching your cartoon, *Harvey Wallbanger*.

ANGUS: Great.

LANCE: We couldn't help noticing that your name isn't in the credits.

ANGUS: Yeah. I try to keep a low profile.

CLAYTON: So you don't want your name in the credits of your own cartoon?

ANGUS: No.

LANCE: So how come you live in a crappy house?

ANGUS: What?

CLAYTON: We went by your house. It's not a rich guy's house.

ANGUS: It's the house my parents picked.

LANCE: You're a liar.

ROGUE: No, he's not.

CLAYTON: How do you know?

ROGUE: 'Cause he's not. He draws all the time.

CLAYTON: Have you seen his drawings?

(*Beat.*)

ROGUE: Well . . . no.

LANCE: So? Don't you see? He's scamming us.

ROGUE: He's got pictures right here. He was drawing just now. He can show you. Show them, Angus.

ANGUS: No.

ROGUE: What?

ANGUS: They're private. They're mine.

FELIX: But aren't you going to put them on TV anyway?

ANGUS: Doesn't matter. They're not ready yet, and I don't want to show them.

FELIX: But why?

ANGUS: I don't need to tell you why. That's just how I feel.

ROGUE: But don't you want to prove yourself?

ANGUS: I don't need to prove myself. And if you were my friends, you'd just believe me.

ROGUE: Yeah, but . . .

ANGUS: You don't trust me?

LANCE: I don't. I think you're a liar.

ANGUS: You're going to side with him?

FELIX: Maybe if you just showed us . . . You guys, I'm sure he's not lying. Why would he lie?

CLAYTON: Well, let's see . . . He has people paying attention to him all the time, people buy him stuff, girls like him . . . Don't you get it, Felix? He's been making us look like idiots!

FELIX: No, you guys. It doesn't make sense.

LANCE: Yes, it does. Don't you see? You've never seen his drawings. His name isn't in the cartoon. Why would a famous guy come to this school? You'd go live in New York or L.A. or something.

FELIX: But they bothered him there.

CLAYTON: They would bother him *less* in a big city. There are more famous people there. It's not a big deal for city kids to see a famous person.

FELIX: But . . . that does sort of make sense.

ANGUS: Well, you guys can think whatever you want. I'm out of here.

ROGUE: Come on, Angus. Just show them your pictures.

ANGUS: Great. You don't believe me either. Really nice, Rogue. Well, nice knowing you.

(ANGUS exits.)

TALK BACK!

1. Has anyone ever made an assumption about your personality based on your looks and guessed wrong? Why do you think that happened?

2. Do you think Angus is telling the truth or lying?

3. What would you do if you thought a friend of yours lied to you?

4. Are there any types of people you feel intimidated by based on how they dress or look? Why or why not?

5. Do you choose your friends based on how similar they are to you? Is this a natural tendency? Is it a good tendency?

6. Is Lance smart? Cautious about strangers? Jealous?

DON'T TELL

4F, 4M

WHO

FEMALES	MALES
Dora	Eddy
Darcy	Ned
Karen	Pete
Leila	Tim

WHERE School.

WHEN Present day.

Everyone in this play, especially Leila, has to believe what he or she is doing is right. Be careful not to judge your character. Try to see the situation from his or her viewpoint.

Cheating, tattling, and keeping secrets are all big issues. Think about where you stand on one of these issues and write a scene from the *opposite* viewpoint. See if you can see things from the other side!

Scene 1: Little Things

PETE: Keep quiet, Leila.

LEILA: Why should I?

DORA: Because he didn't do his homework. *(Beat, as if listening to a teacher offstage.)* I didn't say anything, Ms. Granger. *(Quietly.)* Jeez, you guys got me in trouble. *(Beat.)* That wasn't me talking, Ms. Granger. *(Quietly.)* I hate you guys!

LEILA: Excuse me, Ms. Granger? I think you should know that Dora was talking. She was asking Pete why he was talking. So it was really his fault, not Dora's.

PETE: What's wrong with you?

LEILA: Ms. Granger, Pete is not being nice to me.

(Beat.)

PETE: But, Ms. Granger, I didn't—But—It's not fair! I didn't do anything!

DORA: And I was just—Leila was talking, too!

(Beat.)

PETE: Leila, you are so dead.

(A bell rings.)

LEILA: Wait, Ms. Granger! You forgot to collect our homework.

PETE: You are so, so, so dead!

LEILA: I'm not scared of you.

(DORA stands up.)

DORA: Leila, you really have got to stop doing this. You're such a tattletale. It's annoying and no one wants to be your friend.

LEILA: But if people are doing something wrong, I don't see why I should keep quiet.

DORA: Sometimes it's better to keep your mouth shut. You're not God or something. You don't get to judge everyone. You're not perfect, either. I know you think so, but you're not. You were talking in class, too. Why did you have to get Pete and me in trouble? What was the point? Can't you ever just let something go?

LEILA: I just don't see why I should.

DORA: And what difference would it make if Ms. Granger didn't collect our homework today?

LEILA: But I did my homework.

DORA: So what if you did your homework! Can't you do something nice for someone else for once? You had better make sure you never, ever, *ever* make a mistake in your whole life because everyone is going to be so happy to see *you* get into trouble for once. Just don't even talk to me anymore, Leila. I'm sick of you. If you'll excuse me, I guess I have to clean the blackboards in the other classrooms now.

(DORA exits.)

PETE: Well, Leila. Looks like you just lost another friend.

LEILA: If she can't understand the difference between right and wrong, I don't need her as a friend.

PETE: What are you talking about?

LEILA: It's wrong to talk in class and it was wrong of you to threaten me and it's wrong to lie. So you both deserve what you got.

PETE: You are officially the craziest girl on the face of the earth. No, scratch that. You're officially the craziest human, animal, plant, living thing on the face of the earth!

LEILA: Well if being a good person makes me crazy, then I guess I'm crazy. Only I, personally, think you're the crazy one for not doing your homework and getting into trouble all the time.

PETE: I get in trouble all the time because *you* get me into trouble. Because you just can't keep your big mouth shut. Didn't anyone ever tell you that no one likes a snitch?

LEILA: I'm honest, not a snitch.

PETE: You're more than honest. Honest is just when you don't tell lies about yourself. A snitch is someone who says things about other people on purpose to get them in trouble.

LEILA: I feel sorry for you, Pete. You just don't get

it. It wouldn't even matter if you got your homework done. It's your own fault you get into trouble. It has nothing to do with me. You wish it did. You're just mad because you know you deserve what you're getting. Besides, I never understood why as kids we're always taught to tell the truth then when we do, people get mad. The truth is the truth. Whether it's about you or someone else. Honest is honest. You can't change the definition to suit your own rules. You didn't do your homework. You were bothering people in class. So you should be punished. By the way, shouldn't you be cleaning the blackboards?

PETE: Someday, Leila, all this will come back to haunt you.

LEILA: Not if I have anything to do with it.

PETE: You'd better hope you're as perfect as you think you are.

LEILA: I am.

(PETE exits.)

LEILA: What is wrong with everybody?

(DARCY and KAREN enter.)

DARCY: Leila! Hi!

LEILA: Hi!

KAREN: How come you're not outside for recess?

LEILA: You don't even want to know. Dora and Pete were complaining that they got into trouble.

DARCY: Oh. Well. I guess you want to go outside now.

LEILA: I guess. So what are you guys inside for?

KAREN: Oh, no reason. We just didn't want to be outside.

DARCY: Um, we were just going to get a head start on our homework.

LEILA: That's smart. Maybe I'll do the same thing!

KAREN: Well . . .

(KAREN and DARCY exchange a look.)

DARCY: It's really nice outside, though. You might not want to miss out on the sunshine.

KAREN: We were only going to do our homework because we have somewhere to go tonight, so we won't be able to do it later.

LEILA: Yeah, but it would be nice for me to have it done. Then I can have the whole night to relax. I've been wanting to finish a book, too.

DARCY: But . . . Leila . . . OK. To be honest, we were going to have a private conversation.

LEILA: About what?

KAREN: It's private.

LEILA: You can tell me. I can keep a secret.

DARCY: Are you serious?

LEILA: What?

DARCY: You've never kept a secret in your life.

LEILA: I've kept lots of secrets.

KAREN: No you haven't. You tell everyone everything.

DARCY: No offense, but you're a tattletale.

LEILA: I . . . I thought we were friends.

DARCY: Well, we are, but there's certain things we can't tell you.

KAREN: Because of the tattling.

LEILA: So you're going to do something bad.

KAREN: Not *bad*. Just something we don't want everyone to know about.

LEILA: So then you can tell me.

DARCY: No, we can't.

LEILA: Please?

KAREN: We can't.

DARCY: Can you please leave us so we can talk privately, Leila?

LEILA: Come on, you guys! You can trust me. I really can keep a secret.

KAREN: Leila, we can't trust you. I'm sorry. There are just some things that we need to say and do when you're not around.

DARCY: We have some secrets between us that Karen doesn't know.

LEILA: We do?

KAREN: You do?

DARCY: Yeah!

LEILA: Well, OK.

KAREN: We'll see you later.

LEILA: OK.

(LEILA exits.)

KAREN: You have some secrets with her that I don't know about?

DARCY: No. Are you kidding? You can't tell her anything unless you want the entire school to know it, too.

KAREN: Sometimes she's OK and I almost like her. Then other times . . .

DARCY: I know. She just can't keep her mouth shut.

KAREN: She still thinks we're best friends with her.

DARCY: I feel bad about that. But what are we supposed to do? She's just too bossy, and she thinks she's always right. There's some stuff I just don't want to tell her.

KAREN: I know. Because there are things you just don't want the whole world to know. I don't hate her or anything . . . You just can't be around her all the time. So! Let's talk. What's going on, Darcy?

DARCY: You promise not to tell?

KAREN: Definitely. I wouldn't do that to you.

(Unnoticed by KAREN and DARCY, LEILA sneaks back onstage to listen in on their conversation.)

Scene 2: Big Things

TIM: What did you get on the test?

KAREN: I got a B plus.

DARCY: Me, too! I guess great minds think alike.

EDDY: No way! I got a C.

NED: You two got the same grade on the last test, too, didn't you?

KAREN: We're best friends.

DARCY: We think alike.

LEILA: You think alike?

KAREN: Yeah.

LEILA: I wouldn't think even best friends could get the same grade on *every* test.

DARCY: Well, that's how it is.

NED: You must have some kind of psychic connection. Like twins.

LEILA: Then how come I do better than you two? I'm best friends with you, too.

KAREN: I guess Darcy and I are just closer.

DARCY: More alike.

TIM: Take it easy, Leila. Not everything has to be a federal issue. It's just a coincidence.

EDDY: Yeah, officer. Back off. It's no crime to get the same grade on a test.

PETE: Don't you have somewhere else to be? I think someone somewhere in the world is chewing gum in school. You'd better go find them or they might get away with it!

EDDY: Good one, Pete!

LEILA: Shut up, you guys. You're such babies.

EDDY: And you're so mature.

LEILA: Yeah, I am.

TIM: Excuse me if I don't want to be old yet.

PETE: Yeah, who wants to be old? I never want to be old. I mean, I hate school and all, but I don't want to work in a bank, either. How boring would that be? If I *have* to have a job when I'm older, I'm going to be a sportscaster. And the homework for that is to watch sports on TV. So what's the point of school? Who really learns anything anyway? I mean, let's look at Leila here. Sure, she knows stuff, she gets A's, but does she really *know* anything? She certainly doesn't know how to deal with people. I mean, who actually likes her?

LEILA: People like me, moron.

NED: He's just using you as an example.

LEILA: People like me!

PETE: No, see, they don't. No one likes you. So sure, you know some dumb stuff about math and science and history, but what about things that are actually useful like getting along with other people? I mean, who's going to marry a tattletale know-it-all like you?

LEILA: First of all, maybe I'm not going to get married.

NED: Well, duh!

LEILA: Because I don't want to! Second of all, I'm not a tattletale!

PETE: See? You proved my point. You don't even know you're a tattletale. So being smart in school and getting good grades didn't help you at all really. You're as dumb or even dumber than the rest of us!

LEILA: I hate all of you!

(LEILA starts to exit.)

PETE: I thought you liked honesty!

LEILA: You're not being honest; you're being mean!

PETE: Are you going to go cry to the teacher?

LEILA: Drop dead!

(LEILA exits.)

NED: Whoa. That was intense.

PETE: She deserves that.

TIM: She thinks she knows everything.

EDDY: I don't know how you girls can stand her.

KAREN: We just kind of can't get rid of her.

DARCY: She's stuck to us.

NED: I bet she got a B on the test or something. She's jealous of you guys or something.

TIM: Maybe she actually knows you don't like her anymore.

DARCY: That would almost be a relief.

(LEILA reenters.)

LEILA: Karen and Darcy, I just want you two to know that I know.

KAREN: What are you talking about?

LEILA: I know. What you did.

DARCY: You sound crazy, Leila. We don't know what you're talking about.

LEILA: I heard you two talking in the classroom the other day during recess.

KAREN: What?

DARCY: Were you eavesdropping?

KAREN: We told you we were having a private conversation.

DARCY: We purposely didn't want you around!

LEILA: Well, I forgot something so I came back.

EDDY: What did you forget?

NED: What difference does that make?

KAREN: No, that's a good question. What did you forget?

LEILA: I can't remember now.

KAREN: Because you're lying!

PETE: Leila! Lying? No! The world is coming to an end!

LEILA: Shut up, Pete. This has nothing to do with you.

DARCY: It also has nothing to do with you, Leila! Just leave it alone. It's none of your business.

LEILA: Well, that's really funny because I could have actually helped you.

DARCY: How? By telling everyone?

LEILA: By *teaching* you. I don't know why you guys hate me so much now.

KAREN: Because of things like this, Leila. This is personal. Don't say anymore. It's none of anyone's business.

LEILA: But it's wrong!

TIM: Does anyone know what's going on here?

KAREN: No! And they shouldn't.

DARCY: Leila, please don't say anymore. We're friends.

LEILA: Are we? I heard what you two just said about me. It doesn't sound like we're friends.

KAREN: We were just annoyed.

DARCY: Leila, sometimes it's really hard to be around you.

EDDY: This just became a really girlie conversation. Anyone for tag football outside?

NED: Let's go while we can.

PETE: I think I might stay and watch the fight.

KAREN: Get lost, Pete.

PETE: Whatever.

   (TIM, EDDY, NED, and PETE exit.)

KAREN: See? Even Pete can listen. Even he knows when to get out of the way.

LEILA: You guys are mean and now you're cheaters, too. I hope you're proud of yourselves.

KAREN: Well, if you listened to our conversation, then you'd know that there's a reason for it.

DARCY: Karen was just trying to help me.

LEILA: Maybe you should tell the teacher instead of cheating on tests.

DARCY: Oh, that sounds like a great idea. So I can be put back into another grade or something. Leila, did it ever occur to you that you don't know everything? You don't always know what's best for other people. Everything isn't black and white. Sometimes things are complicated. And this is complicated. And if I have to talk about it—which I guess I do since you eavesdropped on our conversation—then I guess I have to tell you that this whole thing is embarrassing to me. It's not what I want. I don't want it to be this way. I just can't work fast enough. I'm not stupid. I just have trouble reading, OK? Karen understands that this doesn't mean I *couldn't* do well on my tests on my own. I could. I just can't work fast enough. So it's not cheating. And if you were ever a friend to me, if you even know what the word "friend" means, you'd keep your mouth shut. I mean it. This is serious. This is my whole life. This is the difference between staying in this grade or getting dropped to lower grade and going into a dummy class. So just don't say anything, Leila.

LEILA: Why should I act like your friend? You don't even like me. You're two-faced.

KAREN: You make us be like that! You're always acting better than everyone else. Leila, this is your chance to prove that you *are* our friend. You said you could keep a secret. This is an important one. Prove to us that you can put friendship over being right all the time. Don't say anything. Keep this between us.

LEILA: But this is cheating. This is a big thing. I think the teacher would want to know. I mean, are you going to keep doing this forever? Are you going to go all through school up until you graduate cheating off of Karen, Darcy? If you tell the teacher, she might be able to help.

DARCY: Leila, are you going to be our friend or not? This is your last chance to prove yourself. If you tell on me, I will never forgive you. You will cease to exist.

LEILA: This isn't talking in class, Darcy! Seriously! You can't ask me to keep this a secret.

KAREN: We can and we are. Do it for Darcy. We're your only friends now, Leila. Please, if we were ever your friends, you have to keep this a secret!

TALK BACK!

1. What would you do in Leila's situation? Would you tell the teacher or would you keep silent? Support your viewpoint.

2. Do you think tattling is right sometimes? All the time? Never?

3. Can you think of a situation where it would be OK to cheat or is it always wrong?

4. Can you think of a situation where it would be important to tell on someone?

5. Are you good at keeping secrets? Why or why not?

6. Would you want to be Leila's friend? If you could give Leila some advice, what would it be?

CHRISTMAS SNAIL

4F, 6M

WHO

FEMALES
> Brioni
> Liz
> Marilyn
> Rick
> Marcel
> Mom

MALES
> Ashton
> Dad
> Kevin
> Luka

WHERE Scene 1: School; Scene 2: The Green home.

WHEN Present day.

🎭 Make sure you don't "play the end." This means no one can suspect the truth about Marcel until it is revealed at the end (so it comes as a surprise!).

✍ To come up with this title, I put a bunch of random words in a hat and pulled two out. Try this same method: choose your random title and see if you can create a play around it.

Scene 1: Welcome to America

ASHTON: *(Depressed.)* Hi, guys.

RICK: Hey, what's going on?

LIZ: Why so sad?

ASHTON: No reason.

LUKA: Who's this guy?

ASHTON: Oh, him. He's Marcel. He's French. I have to show him around.

KEVIN: How come?

ASHTON: He's like an exchange student. For some reason, my parents got him.

MARCEL: Hi!

MARILYN: You can speak English!

ASHTON: He can only say hi.

MARCEL: Hello!

LUKA: Not *only* hi.

ASHTON: Right, right. Hello, too.

LIZ: What do you mean your parents got him?

RICK: Yeah, did they buy him or something?

ASHTON: For some stupid reason, they told someone or other that we'd let him live with us.

KEVIN: He lives with you?

MARILYN: He's kind of cute.

LIZ: Marilyn! Don't say that!

MARILYN: He doesn't understand English, right? We can say whatever we want.

RICK: Are you sure he's not faking?

KEVIN: Let's test him.

MARILYN: Don't be mean.

LIZ: He's not going to be mean. Are you?

KEVIN: Nah.

LUKA: Hello.

MARCEL: Hello! Hi!

LUKA: My skin is purple.

MARCEL: Yes.

LIZ: He knows another word! Are you sure he can't speak English?

LUKA: He agreed that my skin is purple.

KEVIN: This is great! You could blame everything you

ever do wrong on him. You won't ever get in trouble for anything ever again!

ASHTON: He's not staying for my whole life. He's just staying a few months. He'd better not be staying my whole life.

MARILYN: I'm Marilyn and this is Liz.

MARCEL: Hello, Marilyn. Liz. *(Points to himself.)* Marcel.

MARILYN: Hello, Marcel.

MARCEL: Hello. *(Speaking slowly and carefully.)* I . . . want . . . to speak English.

LIZ: He's getting good!

MARCEL: Hello!

LIZ: Hello!

MARILYN: He's friendly.

ASHTON: This is just not fair. My parents came home one night with him. They got him at the airport. No one ever told me. No one said a word to me. They said they did. At least they said they thought they told me, but they didn't. This is something I'd remember. "Ashton, you're going to have to share your room for a few months with some random guy who doesn't speak English."

LUKA: You have to share your room with him?

ASHTON: I have to share my room with him! And he gets all the advantages, even though it's *my* room. I'm sleeping in a foldout cot. I have to get up first in the morning so Marcel here can sleep in.

MARCEL: Hi, Ashton.

ASHTON: Shut up. And my parents take his side on everything. They take him places. This weekend my dad took Marcel to a baseball game and not me!

MARCEL: Ah, baseball!

ASHTON: See? It's unfair! He's like the son my dad's always wanted. They ignore me my whole life, and this French guy comes along and suddenly they're, like, superparents! Give me a break. Marcel?

MARCEL: Oui?

ASHTON: I hate you.

MARCEL: Yes!

KEVIN: Ha, ha. That's pretty funny. Marcel?

MARCEL: Yes. Hello.

KEVIN: You have a monkey face.

MARCEL: Yes?

KEVIN: Yes!

MARILYN: Don't be mean.

LIZ: He can't help that he's from another country. And he can't help that your parents are nicer to him, Ashton. It's their fault, not his. You could be a really big help to him! It must be scary being in a new country and being surrounded by people you don't know who speak a totally different language. Imagine not understanding anything anyone said! I think Marcel is very brave. Marcel brave! Can you say that Marcel? Marcel brave!

RICK: You're going to make him talk like Frankenstein.

LIZ: Frankenstein is the doctor, not the monster. And Marcel *is* going to talk like Frankenstein. I can tell he's intelligent already!

ASHTON: Whoop-dee-do. He said yes and hello.

MARCEL: Liz and Marilyn . . . pretty.

KEVIN: I'm going to puke.

MARILYN: You are so smart, Marcel!

LIZ: Well, if you boys are not going to be nice to Marcel and teach him English, Marilyn and I will. I think he's sweet. Maybe it would be a good lesson for you, Ashton, to try not being a spoiled brat. I just don't believe that your life is so terrible. You have everything you need—a roof over your head, food, an education—how can you possibly complain about sharing a little bit of what you have with Marcel here?

ASHTON: He's not from the middle of nowhere or anything. You're acting like I should feel sorry for him.

He's French; he didn't get brought over here from the African desert or anything. And if I want to hate him, I can.

LIZ: Why don't you be a little bit generous? You might even be friends. Who knows?

ASHTON: We're not going to be friends.

MARILYN: Why not, Ashton?

ASHTON: Because I hate him. You stole my room!

MARILYN: He's ridiculous. Let's go, Marcel.

(MARILYN, LIZ, and MARCEL exit.)

ASHTON: Oooh. Look at me. I'm French. I'm so scared 'cause I don't speak English, and I'm in scary, scary America. What's going to happen to me? Two crazy girls just kidnapped me so they can kiss me. What will I do? I love parents and girls. I'm a big loser! Look at me!

RICK: What are you doing?

(MARCEL enters.)

ASHTON: Being stupid Marcel.

MARCEL: Ashton!

ASHTON: What?

MARCEL: Good-bye!

ASHTON: What?

(LIZ and MARILYN enter.)

MARILYN: Marcel? You disappeared!

MARCEL: Good-bye, Ashton.

LIZ: See how nice he is to you, Ashton?

ASHTON: Whatever. Good-bye.

MARCEL: Good-bye.

(MARCEL, LIZ, and MARILYN exit.)

KEVIN: Do you really think they'll kiss him?

LUKA: Ugh. Who cares?

RICK: He's French. Isn't that what they do?

LUKA: He can have them.

ASHTON: Can you believe all that "Marilyn and Liz . . . so pretty" stuff? Seriously, what is wrong with him? Am I wrong to hate him?

RICK: I can't believe your parents made you share a room with him.

ASHTON: Don't remind me. This is a total disaster. I bet at the end of all this *I* get sent back to France instead of him. Since he's like the son my parents always wanted. You should see him! He's so polite and every-thing.

KEVIN: Maybe he's secretly a serial killer. No one can really be that polite and nice. He'll crack sometime.

ASHTON: Well, great. Now I not only have to worry about him taking over my family, now I also have to worry about him killing me in my sleep. Thanks a lot, Kevin.

KEVIN: That's what I'm here for.

Scene 2: Later, Frenchie

ASHTON: When is he going home?

MOM: Ashton! Behave yourself! It's Christmas.

ASHTON: So?

DAD: Young man, you've done nothing but walk around with a bad attitude for months. I will not stand for that on Christmas.

ASHTON: Why not? You stand for it every other day.

DAD: Are you trying to push my buttons? Because you are pushing my buttons, and I don't think you want to push my buttons if you know what's good for you.

ASHTON: I just want an answer to my question.

MOM: Ashton, you go to your room and think about what you've done until mealtime.

ASHTON: Fine!

(ASHTON exits.)

MOM: What's wrong with him?

DAD: I don't know, but it's going to stop.

MOM: One thing about having Marcel around is that we can see how boys his age are supposed to act; they're capable of behaving like something other than spoiled brats. I'm sorry to say it, but—

DAD: But that's exactly how our son is acting. All I have to do is give Marcel some help with his homework or watch a game with him, and Ashton goes crazy. I don't know what's wrong with him. For Pete's sake, Marcel is in a foreign country! I think it's our duty to help him out with his studies and teach him our customs.

MOM: I was hoping Ashton would help out with that.

DAD: Well, we were all hoping this experience would help him.

MOM: Why can't he understand that we did this for him?

DAD: All he can understand is that we asked him to share his room.

MOM: And why is that such a terrible thing?

DAD: It's not. It's reasonable. I had to share a room with my brother my whole life. Ah, well, kids will be kids.

(MARCEL enters.)

MARCEL: Hello, American family! Can I help?

MOM: Marcel, your English is so excellent now! I'm proud of you.

MARCEL: Thank you. Can I help you?

MOM: Oh, no, Marcel. Oh! Maybe you could tell Ashton it's time for dinner.

MARCEL: Why . . . Why does Ashton hate me? I try to

be like his friends, but he does not like me. Have I done something to offend? Because I want American friends.

(ASHTON enters.)

DAD: Marcel, don't you worry about a thing. Our son is a spoiled brat.

ASHTON: Thanks a lot, Dad. Really nice. Insult me in front of your real son.

DAD: What are you talking about now?

ASHTON: You wish he were your son because he's polite.

DAD: It would be nice if my own son were a little more polite.

ASHTON: Great. Well, at least you admit it now.

MOM: Ashton, no one's admitting anything. Now settle down. It's time to eat. Marcel, would you get Brioni?

MARCEL: Yes, Mrs. Green.

(MARCEL exits.)

MOM: See how calm and nice he is, Ashton?

ASHTON: See how perfect Marcel is, Ashton? Ashton, Marcel makes his bed every day. Why can't you do that? Ashton, why are you such a disaster when Marcel is perfect?

DAD: That's enough. I don't want to hear any more from you, Ashton.

ASHTON: That's just it, don't you see? You never want to hear from me. You never want to listen to me! You always ignore me when I say something you don't like. Why can't you just listen for once? Maybe I'm not perfect like Marcel, but I'm your kid whether you like it or not. How come you don't take me to baseball games, Dad? I'm your son and you never take me anywhere. He's a stranger and he gets the red carpet treatment. That's just—Does this make sense to anyone but me?

DAD: Calm down and sit down, Ashton.

ASHTON: No! I won't calm down. Not until you listen to me. I feel like I'm going crazy sometimes. How come you can't see that you treat him better than me? Even if you don't like me, you're supposed to still take care of me. Or at least pretend to. What makes him so great anyway? He doesn't know you—that's why he's polite. Maybe he yells at his parents, too. Maybe he feels like they ignore him, too. But he's polite to you since he's a guest in a foreign country and he has to be nice because he has nowhere else to go. Plus, you're extra nice to him! Who wouldn't be polite to someone who gave him everything he wanted? *I'd* be nice to you if my life was like that.

(BRIONI enters.)

BRIONI: What's the yelling all about? Let me guess. It's about Marcel living here and how Ashton has to share his room.

ASHTON: It's easy for you to be cool about it since you don't have to share *your* room.

BRIONI: So?

ASHTON: So?

(MARCEL enters.)

MARCEL: Should I enter?

MOM: Come on in and sit down, Marcel. Don't mind all the craziness around here today. Brioni and Ashton, don't upset Marcel.

BRIONI: He's not upset, are you, Marcel?

MARCEL: No.

BRIONI: Do families fight in France?

MARCEL: Yes. Some do.

BRIONI: Does your family fight?

MOM: Brioni! Don't ask him questions like that. Now, Marcel, I made a very special Christmas meal this year. I think you're going to like it very much. I made it especially for you! Tonight we are going to have an authentic French meal!

BRIONI: Mom, you're kidding, right?

ASHTON: What about the turkey?

MOM: This year we're having escargot!

BRIONI: What's that?

DAD: Snails. You're giving us snails, Carol?

MOM: Yes!

DAD: Are there—so are there any American dishes?

MOM: Well, we have side dishes you might recognize. Vegetables.

BRIONI: Tell me you're kidding. Marcel, do you honestly like snails?

MOM: Brioni, don't be insulting! Just because a dish is new to you doesn't mean that it's not delicious. You should learn to try new things.

BRIONI: Is there a salad?

MOM: Yes.

BRIONI: I guess I know what I'm eating.

ASHTON: This is a great Christmas.

DAD: Don't be sarcastic with your mother, Ashton.

ASHTON: Do you want to eat snails?

DAD: I'm sure it's very . . . tasty.

ASHTON: I thought you wanted to show Marcel what America is like. Shouldn't we eat American food then?

MOM: Marcel must be a little homesick by now.

DAD: Did you ever consider that, Ashton?

MOM: We just want to make him feel at home.

BRIONI: When are you going home, Marcel?

MARCEL: Next week.

ASHTON: How come she can ask that and I can't?

DAD: That's it. I've had enough. I'm sorry, honey, I'm sure the snails are wonderful, but I have to leave this table.

MOM: Don't. Don't let him get to you.

DAD: I'm going to take a drive around the block.

(DAD exits.)

BRIONI: Isn't this a merry Christmas. Have you ever been to a merrier one, Marcel?

MOM: Stop asking—Just stop! Oh, I can smell the snails burning!

(MOM exits.)

BRIONI: Seriously, Marcel, do you like snails?

MARCEL: Seriously, Brioni? I hate snails. When I was seven, my mother made me eat snails and I—eh, how do you say?—chucked them up. I never eat snails again. Since we are alone, the three of us, and I'm to leave soon, should I tell everything?

BRIONI: Please do.

MARCEL: I hate American football. I didn't want to

tell your father. I could see he liked telling me about it. Why are the games so long? And why is it considered dangerous when the players wear so much padding? None of this could I understand. And about my family, I have three sisters at home who—how do you say?—drive me up to the ceiling.

ASHTON: Up a wall.

MARCEL: Right. Up a wall. Strange expression. Ashton, I understand I am weight to you.

ASHTON: I think you mean a burden.

MARCEL: Right. A burden. I know—I am sorry for making it hard for you. Sharing your room and your friends. And your parents.

ASHTON: It's not your fault. Sorry to be a jerk.

MARCEL: You have been a large jerk to me.

ASHTON: What?

BRIONI: I'm liking you more and more, Marcel! Why couldn't you be like this the whole time?

MARCEL: I am being honest now.

ASHTON: I'm a jerk.

MARCEL: I could understand English all along. I couldn't speak it well, but I could mostly understand.

ASHTON: So you heard everything—What did I say?

MARCEL: **You said many things about me being stupid and boring and smelling French, and how you hated me—**

ASHTON: Sorry. I was mad.

MARCEL: But I understand. I would have said the same about you.

ASHTON: Thanks?

MARCEL: You're welcome.

ASHTON: I'm really sorry.

MOM: *(Speaking from offstage.)* I'm coming in with the escargot in just a minute! Nobody move!

MARCEL: **If you really want to make up to me . . .**

ASHTON: You mean "make it up" . . .

MARCEL: **you'll eat all of the snails your mother made.**

ASHTON: What?

BRIONI: That's fair.

MARCEL: And humorous.

ASHTON: I couldn't possibly!

BRIONI: Ashton, you called him smelly.

ASHTON: Well, I have been a jerk, but . . .

MARCEL: As you Americans say, "Just do it!"

(MOM enters.)

MOM: Here they are!

(DAD enters.)

DAD: Are we going to have a nice meal now?

ASHTON: Give me the snails.

BRIONI: Merry Christmas, everyone.

MARCEL: I am Jewish.

TALK BACK!

1. Have you ever felt that your parents liked your friends or your siblings more than you? How does that feel?

2. Would you like to visit a foreign country and be away from your family for a few months? Why or why not?

3. How would you feel about going to a country where no one spoke English? Would you find it exciting? Scary? Do you think it would be easy or hard to learn their language?

4. Everyone's told from an early age to share with others. Are you good at sharing or do you hate it? Why?

5. Do you, or have you ever, shared a room? What do you think are the good and bad things about having to share your personal space?

6. Are you an only child or do you have brothers or sisters? Which is better: Having siblings or being an only child? What are the pluses and minuses of each situation?

LOST

3F, 3M

WHO

FEMALES   MALES
- Kendra   Christos
- Renee   Monroe
- Twist   Sherrod

WHERE   Scene 1: A bus station; Scene 2: A prison cell.

WHEN   The near future.

😮   Keep in mind in this play that danger lurks around every corner. Try this exercise: Have one person stand just outside the room (or offstage)—this person symbolizes Danger. Under no circumstances do you want this person to enter the room. The actors onstage must go through the scenes without having this person hear them. If the "Danger" person hears them speaking, he or she enters and the exercise is over. Don't let him or her hear you!

✎   What could be a danger the world might face in the future? Write a play about a threatening futuristic society.

Scene 1: Final Stop

KENDRA: Where are we?

RENEE: I thought you knew where we were going.

KENDRA: You were supposed to help me look for the right stop. I asked you to look.

RENEE: But you said you knew. You said you thought you'd know it when you saw it.

KENDRA: Well, I made a mistake, OK?

RENEE: So now what are we going to do?

KENDRA: I don't know. How should I know?

RENEE: Can we get back on a bus?

KENDRA: We used our tickets. And I don't have any money. Do you?

RENEE: No. Mom gave you the money.

KENDRA: So we have no money.

RENEE: Maybe a driver will be nice to us and let us ride for free.

KENDRA: Are you kidding? No way. We're stuck.

RENEE: Maybe Grandma put us on the wrong bus in the first place.

KENDRA: Maybe. Maybe that's why I never saw our stop. Maybe we didn't go anywhere near it!

RENEE: So we're really, really lost then. We aren't anywhere near home.

KENDRA: We should figure out where we are.

RENEE: But then we'd have to talk to strangers. We don't know if they're dangerous.

KENDRA: Well, how else are we going to figure out how to get home?

RENEE: Kendra, I'm really worried. We can't get a ride in a car with someone.

KENDRA: Of course not. That would be dangerous.

RENEE: We can't get a job to get money.

KENDRA: We're too young.

RENEE: How are we going to get home?

KENDRA: Maybe someone has a cell phone and we can call Mom.

RENEE: But that means we have to talk to a stranger.

KENDRA: Let's try to find someone who looks safe.

RENEE: You can't tell by how someone looks if they're dangerous!

KENDRA: Well, it's our only option now! We're in the

middle of nowhere, Renee. We don't have any idea where we are or how to get home. We have no money. We have to do something! I say we find a girl and ask her to help us.

RENEE: I don't know, Kendra. You still never know . . .

KENDRA: We just have to stick together. I'll do the talking.

(TWIST enters.)

KENDRA: There's a girl!

RENEE: Don't do it, Kendra. There must be another way. We should talk to a bus driver. Maybe they'd understand.

KENDRA: Come on, Renee. It's going to be dark soon. We don't have much time to work this out.

(KENDRA walks over to TWIST. RENEE reluctantly follows.)

KENDRA: Hi!

TWIST: Hi. Do I know you? Because I don't think I do.

KENDRA: No. You don't know us. We're lost. We were hoping maybe you could help us.

TWIST: I doubt it.

KENDRA: Why?

TWIST: I'm lost, too.

RENEE: What?

TWIST: I'm lost, too. I got off at the wrong stop.

RENEE: So did we!

TWIST: I could swear the bus took a different route today. I don't know what I'm going to do. I'm supposed to be having dinner with my cousins right now. I'm supposed to be at my aunt and uncle's house. And I can't go home either, because I don't have enough money and my mom is having a baby. That's why I'm supposed to go to my aunt and uncle's. To be honest, I'm kind of freaking out, so I'm probably not going to be much help to you. I can't even help myself! And for all I know you two are going to rob and kill me now. Well, at least my parents are going to have another kid so they won't miss me too much. So I guess I'm just going to stand here and get murdered because what else can I do? No one's ever going to come looking for me here. No one knows I'm here. I don't even know where here is. And it's going to get cold and dark, so even if you don't kill me, I'll probably freeze to death. I don't want to live on the streets. I don't want to be alone and dirty. So let's just get this over with. Just—just murder me now.

RENEE: You're even more scared than me.

KENDRA: You've got to get a hold of yourself! There's got to be a way back. Where were you going?

TWIST: Mercerville.

RENEE: So were we!

KENDRA: So we should stick together. I'm Kendra, by the way. This is Renee.

RENEE: I can talk for myself.

TWIST: How do I know you're not murderers?

KENDRA: We don't have any weapons.

RENEE: We're kids, too.

TWIST: So?

KENDRA: I guess you just have to trust us.

RENEE: I swear we're not murderers. Cross my heart and hope to die. We were worried that you would be a murderer, too.

TWIST: But you talked to me.

RENEE: That was her idea.

KENDRA: So? What are you going to do . . .

TWIST: I'm Teresa, but everybody calls me Twist. I guess we should stick together. Safety in numbers. It's better than being alone. Do you have any ideas?

(CHRISTOS, MONROE, and SHERROD enter.)

MONROE: Excuse us—

KENDRA: We have no money!

MONROE: No, no, we're not asking for money.

TWIST: They're going to murder us!

RENEE: We know where we are! Our attack dog is around here somewhere with our dad who's an army general!

CHRISTOS: Whoa! Hold up there!

SHERROD: I think you've got the wrong idea. We're not going to rob or kill you. See, we're totally lost. Are you from around here?

TWIST: Yes!

SHERROD: So where are we?

RENEE: We're . . . here.

SHERROD: Where's here?

KENDRA: The bus stop.

SHERROD: That's just it. We got off the bus and now we're lost. We don't know how to get home. Can you help us?

(Beat.)

CHRISTOS: Do you really live here? Because you seem clueless. Where's your dad? Maybe he can help.

RENEE: He's nearby. He'll be here any minute.

MONROE: OK. We'll just wait for him. Do you think he can give us a ride home? We're totally lost.

TWIST: No. No, he couldn't. He's . . . busy.

CHRISTOS: Jeez. OK. Maybe he can at least give us directions.

(Beat.)

MONROE: Where is he exactly?

KENDRA: Over there somewhere.

MONROE: Where?

KENDRA: How should I know?

CHRISTOS: You guys are a little bit touchy. Anyone ever tell you that?

TWIST: *(To RENEE and KENDRA.)* You guys, I'm scared.

RENEE: Me, too.

SHERROD: What are you scared of?

RENEE: What?

SHERROD: What are you scared of? If anyone here should be scared, it's us. We're lost.

TWIST: How do we know that?

SHERROD: Because we just told you that. You girls are acting really weird.

KENDRA: I think we have to tell them.

RENEE: Why?

KENDRA: Because . . . they're waiting for our dad to show up.

TWIST: Let's just go somewhere else.

KENDRA: Where?

TWIST: I don't know. How should I know? This is too much pressure!

KENDRA: Listen, we're lost, too. We didn't want to tell you.

MONROE: Why?

KENDRA: Because you're a bunch of boys. So we were kind of scared.

MONROE: Why do girls always think the worst of boys? We're just people, too. The other day I was walking down the street and I was in a hurry. So I was walking fast. And this lady, she turns around and screams, "Get away from me!" I think she even called me a delinquent. I was just walking fast. I was trying to get somewhere. I didn't want her purse or anything. And now this! You girls do the same thing. We're just kids like you. And we're lost. We just want to get home. You really shouldn't jump to conclusions about people before you know them.

TWIST: But my parents always said not to talk to strangers!

MONROE: Well, of course you shouldn't talk to

strangers, but you should also use some common sense. Do we look dangerous?

RENEE: You can't tell by how someone looks.

MONROE: Do we have guns or knives or anything?

KENDRA: You might.

MONROE: Are we acting scary or overpowering?

TWIST: You're boys. You're stronger than us. I'm scared!

SHERROD: Calm down!

MONROE: There's just no talking to you. Girls don't have any common sense. You just want to think the worst of people. All we did was ask where we were. We'd like to get some directions so we can get home. We don't want anything from you. So just take it easy. If you can't or won't help us, we'll go find someone who will.

KENDRA: Wait!

CHRISTOS: What? We need to get home before dark. Our parents will be worrying.

KENDRA: We should stick together. I just can't help thinking . . . Why did we *all* get lost? Something strange is going on here.

CHRISTOS: I think she's right.

SHERROD: Yeah. Something strange *is* going on here.

Scene 2: Citadel City

CHRISTOS: I wonder what happened to those girls.

SHERROD: I bet they don't have to work like us.

MONROE: Maybe they have to do different work.

CHRISTOS: I wonder how long they've been doing this to kids.

SHERROD: I wonder if we'll ever get home.

MONROE: My parents must be worried about me.

SHERROD: Mine, too.

CHRISTOS: We've got to figure a way out of this.

SHERROD: But they're filming us all the time.

MONROE: And there are guards everywhere.

CHRISTOS: I know. But there's just got to be a way. There are buses that get kids here, right?

MONROE: Right.

CHRISTOS: So why can't we sneak on one and get out of here again?

SHERROD: Well, first of all, we'd have to get out of the citadel; second of all, we'd have to get on the bus without the bus driver seeing us. I don't see how we can do either of those things.

MONROE: We're in prison for life, and we didn't even do anything wrong!

CHRISTOS: We got on the wrong bus.

MONROE: The punishment hardly fits the crime.

CHRISTOS: There's got to be something we can do. I just have to believe that we can find a way out of here. There's no way that I can spend the rest of my life in this pit. We spend all day mining for diamonds, building fortresses to keep us inside, then we're locked up at night. Sleeping on the floors, crammed in like sardines. Our every move is watched. We get yelled at or beaten if we stop to rest. I'm sick of this! There has to be a way out! How can this happen in this country? Was there a war and no one told us? Are we prisoners? How come no one is coming to save us from this place? Do you think . . . Maybe they are! Maybe our parents are coming to get us. They must miss us by now. Look at all the kids here—someone must miss us! All these kids can't just disappear without a trace with no one missing them! So we just need to wait. We just need to keep going. We need to stay patient. Someone will set us free. Someone will overcome these tyrants.

SHERROD: I don't know, Christos.

MONROE: No one's come here yet. Wouldn't we hear about it if someone's parents came?

CHRISTOS: You don't think . . . Could they do anything to our families to keep them away? Could they be hurting anyone who comes hear here? This is all so confusing. None of this makes sense. There's something we're missing here.

SHERROD: Our parents probably think we just ran away.

CHRISTOS: I hope not! There has to be a way out!

(KENDRA, RENEE, and TWIST crawl in from under the back curtain.)

KENDRA: Careful!

TWIST: Ouch! You stepped on me!

KENDRA: Be quiet!

RENEE: Where—

KENDRA: Oh. Hi again.

MONROE: What are you doing here?

SHERROD: How did you get here?

RENEE: Can you keep a secret?

TWIST: Maybe we shouldn't tell, Renee!

CHRISTOS: Not this again.

KENDRA: Maybe they can help. We could use some help.

MONROE: With what?

KENDRA: We're digging a tunnel out of here. There's a big wall around this place. We're going to dig under it.

SHERROD: With what?

(*KENDRA, RENEE, and TWIST pull spoons out of their pockets.*)

MONROE: Spoons?

RENEE: We're working in the kitchens washing dishes all day long. It's all we could manage to take.

TWIST: We've been digging so long. We thought we were done. We thought we were out. I can't believe we're only here!

KENDRA: So it means we need to dig more. At least we ended up here and not in a guard's room or something. Maybe this is the best thing that could have happened to us. Maybe we can get more help?

RENEE: Will you guys help us get out of here?

TWIST: We hate it here. I never liked washing dishes before, now I *really* hate it! Do you know that the guards get desserts?

MONROE: That is so unfair.

TWIST: I know!

CHRISTOS: Well, I'm in.

SHERROD: We all are. Right, Monroe?

MONROE: Definitely. We have to dig in the mines.

RENEE: Do you have shovels?

KENDRA: Renee, that's brilliant!

RENEE: I know! So do you?

MONROE: We do!

TWIST: Excellent!

CHRISTOS: Wait! Can you tell us what's going on here? Why are we here? Who's keeping us here? How come no one's come to get us?

KENDRA: One question at a time! And keep your voice down. OK. Here's what we've figured out.

RENEE: The guards come to the kitchens to eat and they gossip in front of us like we're invisible.

KENDRA: **They tricked our families into sending us here. They told them this was a special school for talented children. They told our parents not to tell us before we got on the bus because it was going to be a great surprise, an honor. But, obviously, that was a lie! This is a work camp for the government. We're helping to build weapons and fortresses across the world. They're afraid that there's going to be a huge war any day now, and we have to be protected and prepared.**

SHERROD: Why children and not adults?

KENDRA: **They're using children because it's easier to keep us here. Or so they think.**

RENEE: But you left out part of it! What about the parents?

KENDRA: Somehow they're sending fake pictures, letters, and report cards home to our families to show how happy we are here, so they don't come looking for us. And if an adult starts insisting on seeing their kid, the kid gets taken to a dinner with their parents, and some guards pretend they're teachers. The parents go away then, and the kid gets punished—put in a prison and made to send letters telling their parents not to ever come back. They have to tell their families that they never want to see them again. We're not going to take it anymore. We're going home.

TWIST: I never thought I'd miss school.

RENEE: I miss our mom so much.

SHERROD: The government made us prisoners in our own country? This is wrong. We just have to get out. These people are crazy! How can you do this to kids?

MONROE: What happens if we succeed in getting outside the walls?

TWIST: What do you mean?

MONROE: We're in the same place we were before we got here.

SHERROD: Are there guards outside the walls? Will we be caught?

RENEE: We don't know that part.

TWIST: Could we be killed? I never even thought about

that! I just thought we'd be out! I don't want to be killed.

KENDRA: Do you want to die working here? Without ever seeing your family again?

MONROE: Don't you see? We'll still be lost, though. We'll still have no way home.

SHERROD: But we'll be free. We'll have a chance.

KENDRA: I thought that if we can manage to dig out of here, we can do anything. That's the hardest part, right? I'm not scared anymore of sleeping on the streets or walking long distances or being cold.

SHERROD: I agree.

MONROE: But we still don't know what we'll find outside. Maybe people will capture us. Maybe there's no way out.

CHRISTOS: We have to try. We have to see our families. We have to get the other kids out. Don't you see? Every kid here is depending on us to help them out of here. We need to tell the news channels what's going on. We need to stop this now.

SHERROD: We could be heroes!

TWIST: Or we could die!

CHRISTOS: But we have to try. Hand me a shovel.

TALK BACK!

1. Would you try to escape or would you hope to be rescued?

2. What do you think you'd hate most about being a prisoner? What do you think you'd miss most from home?

3. After they dig out of the fortress, what can these characters do to get home? What are the dangers and hardships they face?

4. Are you more of a trusting person or a nontrusting person? Is there a way to judge whether a person is trustworthy or not?

5. Do you think these characters are brave or foolish to try to escape? Why?

6. Could something like this happen in real life? Why or why not?

PIECE OF
THE PIE

2F, 5M

WHO

FEMALES
    Lorna
    Marykate

MALES
    Benny
    Jon
    Louis
    Ray
    Yogi

WHERE Outside, in a park.

WHEN Present day.

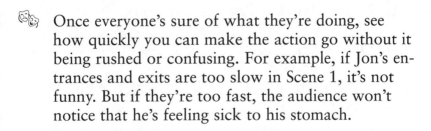 Once everyone's sure of what they're doing, see how quickly you can make the action go without it being rushed or confusing. For example, if Jon's entrances and exits are too slow in Scene 1, it's not funny. But if they're too fast, the audience won't notice that he's feeling sick to his stomach.

Write a sequel: The Case of the Weirdly Dying Old Dudes.

Scene 1: The Pie

(BENNY runs across the stage.)

BENNY: Aaaaaah!

(MARYKATE runs across the stage.)

MARYKATE: Gross! Yuck! Yuck! Yuck!

(RAY walks across the stage.)

RAY: Benny, where are you going? What's going on?

(JON runs across the stage.)

JON: I am never eating pie again!

(LOUIS enters.)

LOUIS: Somebody call the police!

RAY: I showed up late. What's going on?

(YOGI enters.)

YOGI: This is officially the grossest thing I've ever been a witness to.

RAY: What's going on? Who won the pie contest?

(BENNY enters.)

BENNY: Not all the lemonade in the world will wash that out of my mouth! Aaaah!

(BENNY runs offstage.)

LOUIS: Whose could it be?

RAY: What?

YOGI: The pie contest ended—

RAY: Who won?

LOUIS: No one. It just ended.

RAY: Why?

YOGI: Because . . .

LOUIS: Benny found a finger in his pie.

RAY: What!

LOUIS: Benny found a finger in his pie!

RAY: I heard you! I just can't believe it!

YOGI: I know. It's really very disgusting, isn't it?

RAY: Was it human?

LOUIS: What else?

RAY: It could be a monkey's finger.

LOUIS: Where is someone going to get a monkey's finger?

RAY: I don't know. Where is someone going to get a—

YOGI: Could we stop talking about this please?

(*JON enters, looking sick.*)

LOUIS: But this is a crime.

YOGI: So?

LOUIS: Maybe we should solve it!

RAY: "The Mystery of the Missing Finger." I like it!

(**When he hears the word "finger," JON covers his mouth as though he's going to be sick and runs offstage.**)

LOUIS: What's his problem? He didn't even find it.

YOGI: Well, he did eat a lot of pie.

(*LORNA enters.*)

LORNA: Maybe he knows something. Maybe guilt is making him sick.

YOGI: Hi, Lorna. What's up?

LORNA: I'm solving this mystery of the missing finger.

RAY: Hey! We were going to do that!

LORNA: Well, I'm not *going* to do it; I *am* doing it.

RAY: We were doing it, too.

LORNA: No you weren't. You were just talking about it.

LOUIS: OK, stop fighting. Maybe we can work together.

LORNA: Maybe. Maybe not.

YOGI: Come on, Lorna. Let us help.

LORNA: Tell you what. You can be my assistants.

RAY: I don't want to be your assistant. I want to be in charge.

LORNA: Too bad.

LOUIS: OK. Whatever. Let's solve this.

LORNA: Fine with me. I'm already halfway there.

YOGI: So you know who did it?

LORNA: No. But I know it's a lady's finger. Most likely an old lady's finger.

LOUIS: How do you know that?

LORNA: I looked at it.

RAY: How does looking at it tell you all that?

(MARYKATE and JON enter.)

LORNA: You see, this is why you're just an assistant detective. The fingernail was painted. The nail was long. The finger was thin. And wrinkled. An old lady finger. In a pie.

(JON runs offstage to puke and MARYKATE faints.)

LORNA: This is why the faint hearted and the weak stomached are not cut out for detective work. Maybe you boys should go home to your mommies now, because this case is going to get a lot uglier. Yes, that's right. Even uglier than an old lady's finger in a blueberry pie. I don't know how, but I can feel it. It feels a little like spinning in circles for a long time then standing still. It makes you a little dizzy and queasy. For you see, the obvious answer to this mystery is that a worker in the pie factory lost his finger. However, since we have a lady's finger—

MARYKATE: Hello? I fainted here. Isn't anyone going to help me?

RAY: No.

YOGI: Lorna is telling a story!

MARYKATE: I just want to say on the record that all of you stink!

LORNA: Excuse me. Are you done complaining now?

MARYKATE: You're bossy.

LORNA: Done now?

MARYKATE: I guess so.

(MARYKATE goes back to lying on the ground motionless.)

LORNA: As I was saying, since it was a lady's finger in the pie—

LOUIS: But ladies can work in pie factories.

LORNA: I know that. That's not my point.

RAY: What is your point then?

LORNA: **If you'd be quiet, I'd tell you the rest. My point is that an *old* lady wouldn't be working in a pie factory.**

(*JON walks in.*)

LORNA: This was one wrinkled-up, old finger.

(*JON sighs and walks out immediately.*)

LORNA: **This is not the finger of a factory worker. This finger didn't simply fall off into the pie—**

MARYKATE: Stop it. This story is so disgusting.

YOGI: It's disgusting because it's true.

LORNA: **This finger was *placed* in the pie.**

LOUIS: Who would put a finger in a pie on purpose?

RAY: And why?

YOGI: And how?

RAY: And whose finger is it?

YOGI: Doesn't she miss her finger?

LORNA: These are all questions we must answer.

MARYKATE: *(Stands.)* Well, not me. I've had about enough of this. I'm leaving and you can't stop me. *(Begins to exit.)* Don't even try to stop me. *(Exits further, then stops.)* Isn't anyone going to try to stop me?

RAY: No.

MARYKATE: No one?

LOUIS: No.

MARYKATE: Last call . . .

YOGI: No thanks.

MARYKATE: Fine!

(MARYKATE exits.)

YOGI: So how are we going to figure all this out?

LORNA: We are going to use . . . our brains!

(BENNY enters suddenly.)

BENNY: I found a finger in my pie! It was in my mouth! What am I going to do? How can I ever forget this and move on with my life? I can't! Not all the money in the world will make this any better. I'm going to have this memory forever! Now I'll never be able to eat again. And I like eating! I was going to win that pie-eating contest! I was so close. Now all my hopes and dreams are ruined. Ruined! Someday maybe I'll have a family and my wife will try to be nice to me since I'm such a great husband and father and she'll make me a pie and I'll have to tell her, "Sorry, wife, I can't eat pie anymore because once I found a finger in one!" And she'll cry and I'll say I'm sorry. Then I'll try to eat it, but I can't! I can't! And my wife will leave me and take the kids and I'll lose my job because I'm so sad. Plus I've lost loads of weight since I can't eat pie any more even though it's my most favorite food. My pants will be all saggy on me so no one else will want to marry me—My whole life is ruined because of this stupid finger! What am I going to do?

LOUIS: You could sue the pie company.

BENNY: Now there's a good idea! I'll sue the pie company and all the people who work there and the trucking company that delivered the pies and the store they bought the pies from and the people in charge of the pie-eating contest! That's the only way I'll feel better.

LORNA: Well, it should make you feel better to know that we're going to find out who did this and why. Then you won't need to sue as many people.

BENNY: I'm still suing everybody. Someone's got to pay for my pain and suffering!

LORNA: Well, we're still going to solve this mystery. Right, assistants?

YOGI: But it's lunchtime.

RAY: Let's get a snack first.

LOUIS: We can start on this later.

LORNA: Fine.

(LORNA, RAY, YOGI, and LOUIS exit.)

BENNY: Wait for me!

Scene 2: The Piece

LORNA: I have a theory about who committed the crime of the finger in the pie.

YOGI: What's your theory?

LORNA: My theory is that it was . . . Benny!

BENNY: Me? Why would I put a finger in my pie? I had a finger in my mouth! I nearly broke my teeth on the big ring she was wearing. Why would I do that to myself? It was disgusting.

LOUIS: Yeah. Why would anyone do that on purpose?

LORNA: You saw how excited he was about suing the pie company.

RAY: Yeah. It was you!

BENNY: No, it wasn't!

RAY: Yes, it was!

BENNY: No—

LORNA: OK. Why wasn't it you?

BENNY: Because I like to eat pie, not fingers. If it were me, I wouldn't have actually . . . don't you get how gross that was? Really, really, really gross! Not something anyone would do on purpose!

LORNA: OK. Let's say for now that it wasn't Benny. Who died in town in the last few weeks?

LOUIS: Um, there was Mr. Armstrong who had a heart attack when he saw raccoons in his trash cans. . .

YOGI: Mr. McGraw was electrocuted on an electric fence.

RAY: Old man Henderson crashed his pickup to avoid hitting a family of ducks in the road.

BENNY: That's a lot of people.

LORNA: But none of them are old ladies. There must be others.

RAY: I still think it was Benny.

YOGI: Me, too.

BENNY: You guys!

LORNA: Let's focus now on whose finger it could be.

LOUIS: Hey! Jon's grandma died.

LORNA: We need Jon. Ray, go get Jon.

RAY: *(Screaming.)* JON!

LORNA: I could have done that.

(JON enters.)

JON: What?

RAY: Did your grandma die?

JON: Yeah. So?

BENNY: Was her finger in my pie?

JON: No! I don't know. How should I know?

YOGI: Yeah, how should he know?

LORNA: Did your grandma wear nail polish?

JON: I don't know.

LOUIS: He doesn't know.

LORNA: I think he does. I repeat: Did your grandma wear hot pink nail polish!

JON: I don't know! I'm a guy!

LORNA: You do know, Jon! Answer me or you'll have to answer to the police!

JON: Yes, OK, yes! She did!

LORNA: Ah-ha!

LOUIS: But that doesn't mean anything.

YOGI: Sure it does.

LOUIS: What?

YOGI: I don't know. But Lorna knows. Right, Lorna?

LORNA: Right. That means that it was Jon's grandma's finger in the pie.

JON: I'm gonna be sick.

LORNA: No, you're not!

JON: Yes, I am!

(JON runs offstage.)

LORNA: Ray, go get the suspect.

RAY: Could I at least wait until he's done puking?

LORNA: OK.

(MARYKATE enters and sits.)

BENNY: But why would Jon put his grandma's finger in my pie? We're friends.

MARYKATE: You got Jon in trouble for talking in class the other day and he was just laughing at a joke you made. He covered for you and you let him take the punishment. You didn't even help him write "I will not talk in class" a hundred times. That wasn't very nice and I bet he doesn't like you for that.

BENNY: Enough to put his grandma's finger in my pie? That doesn't seem right. After all, that happens all the time in class. I'll say something, Jon will laugh, and he'll get in trouble. It happens every day practically.

MARYKATE: Maybe he just couldn't take it anymore. Maybe he cracked up. Maybe he secretly hates you and your jokes. Maybe he wanted you to eat his grandma's finger.

RAY: Yeah, sure!

YOGI: It doesn't sound right to me.

LOUIS: If Jon's always hated Benny . . . still, it doesn't seem to add up.

LORNA: We need Jon back here.

RAY: I'll get the suspect.

(RAY exits and reenters with JON.)

LORNA: Jon, we've had enough of the runaround. It's time for you to fess up. Maybe we'll even go easy on you.

JON: You're not the police.

LORNA: Who do you see every day in school? The police or us?

YOGI: She makes a good point.

JON: I see you guys.

BENNY: So did you put that finger in my pie because you secretly hate me?

JON: No!

LOUIS: But you did put the finger in his pie!

JON: Well . . . yes!

MARYKATE: Jon, that is so disgusting! Why? Was it because one time Benny said that you still had a nightlight?

JON: You told people that?

BENNY: No!

MARYKATE: Yes, you did. But everybody knew it already.

LORNA: So let's move on! About the finger—

JON: I can't believe you did that, Benny.

BENNY: At least I didn't stick my grandma's dead finger in your mouth.

LOUIS: OK! Let's all take it easy.

RAY: Sit down, Jon. You're under investigation.

YOGI: Ray, I think you might be enjoying this too much.

LORNA: OK! Everyone quiet! I want to hear Jon's explanation for this.

JON: OK. Fine. You want to know how my grandma's finger got into Benny's pie in the pie-eating contest? Well. OK. See, my grandma always used to make the pies for the pie-eating contest. She won a bunch of awards for it, too. She made the best-tasting pies. Then one year, they decided to go with pies from a factory instead. Said she was too expensive. Said they didn't need homemade pies because no one was even tasting them. They were just stuffing them down. So Grandma was mad about that. In her will, she said that when she died she wanted me to put her finger in one of the pies. Ruin the pie contest so she could get her revenge. So . . . I had to! I didn't want to. I had to cut off her finger and put it in the pie. It's the worst thing I ever had to do. But if I didn't, I thought she'd haunt me for life! Anyway, I didn't think Benny would mind since he's always talking about wanting money and suing people. I thought he could sue the pie people, and everybody would be happy. I just didn't count on it being so disgusting. I've been sick for about six hours now. This is just terrible.

LORNA: So it was your grandma's dying wish?

JON: Yes!

BENNY: And you wanted to help me sue the pie people?

JON: Yes!

BENNY: You really are my best friend! Thanks!

JON: No problem.

MARYKATE: So the mystery is solved!

LORNA: Not quite! What happened to her wedding ring?

JON: What do you mean?

LORNA: Benny said he nearly broke his teeth on her ring.

JON: Right. She had her ring on her finger when it went into the pie.

LORNA: But when I inspected her finger, the ring was gone!

JON: Who would do that?

LOUIS: That would be a seriously sick thing to do. Maybe it just fell off.

LORNA: I don't think so.

YOGI: Who would take it?

LORNA: Someone who needs attention. Someone who likes shiny things. Someone who—

MARYKATE: OK. It was me. I wanted it. And it was off the finger, just lying on the table. So I picked it up and cleaned it off. It was pretty.

JON: How dare you take my grandma's ring!

MARYKATE: You took her *finger*. Which is worse?

JON: Give it back, thief!

MARYKATE: Finders, keepers.

JON: You're evil.

MARYKATE: I know you are, but what am I?

YOGI: She makes a good argument there.

JON: Give it back!

MARYKATE: Why should I?

JON: It was my grandma's!

MARYKATE: You guys always ignore me! Now you want something from me, and I'm supposed to listen to you?

Maybe if you paid more attention to me, I'd give your ring back, Jon.

LOUIS: Maybe if you weren't so dramatic we'd pay attention to you more. You're always overdoing it. If something is silly, you laugh so hard you wheeze. Do you really have to clap your hands and throw your hair around, too? It's too much. And when you're sad, you have to weep and wail, holding onto people like you can't stand up. Then today, when you were grossed out, you had to try to be sicker than Jon. And you pretended to faint!

MARYKATE: I fainted for real!

LOUIS: No, you didn't! You faked it. You fake everything. So why should we pay attention to you? And how does us ignoring you mean that you deserve Jon's grandma's ring? If you want to punish us, punish us. But you should give his grandma back her ring. She probably wanted that in that pie.

JON: I don't know if she was that specific—

LOUIS: The point is, Marykate, if you want attention you should go about it in a normal way. Right now, you're too annoying. Try being nice and normal. I'm saying this to try to be helpful, so don't poison me or anything.

MARYKATE: I wouldn't do that.

YOGI: She wouldn't do that.

RAY: So I guess we solved the mystery—or mysteries!

BENNY: And we're all friends.

MARYKATE: Only if you're nice.

YOGI: Are you going to give the ring back, Marykate?

JON: That's OK. I don't want it.

LORNA: Now to find out why all the old men of this town are dying in really weird ways. A detective's job is never done!

TALK BACK!

1. Do you think you'd be a good detective? Why or why not?

2. Would you do what Jon did, if it meant doing your grandma's dying wish?

3. If you had to enter an eating contest, what kind of food would you want to eat and why?

4. Do you think Marykate should keep the ring or give it back? Why or why not?

5. Do you think Benny should sue everyone? Why or why not?

6. How can an actor look sick without actually being sick?

BOYS VS. GIRLS

5F, 5M

WHO

FEMALES	MALES
Bella	Corey
Lisa	Jim
Melanie	Roger
Posy	Spike
Val	Walton

WHERE The schoolyard.

WHEN Present day.

🎭 Really listen and focus on whoever's talking. This will make the relationships and conversations seem real and active.

✎ Write a scene about an argument you had in your life. Feel free to change some of the details. See if you can make the dialogue sound like actual everyday speech. As an experiment, try secretly copying down conversations your friends have. Make sure they don't catch you doing it! This can help you see how people really talk. It's surprising sometimes how little sense we actually make sometimes!

Scene 1: Boys

SPIKE: So did you see that show about sharks on TV yesterday?

JIM: When was it on? Man, I missed it.

COREY: Sharks are so cool.

ROGER: Did anyone get his arm bitten off?

SPIKE: Almost. It was awesome. Came up really close to the sharks and had all these shots of the jaws coming toward you.

JIM: I love those shots.

COREY: It would be even more awesome if it were 3-D.

JIM: That would be great!

ROGER: It would be best of all if someone got his arm bitten off.

WALTON: I hate sharks. Sharks stink.

COREY: What?

JIM: You've got to be joking. Sharks are the best!

WALTON: I don't like them.

SPIKE: Scared?

WALTON: No. **I just don't see the big deal. If you've seen it once, you've seen it a billion times. Ooo, look** how scary it is. The shark is swimming. The shark is circling the cage with the cameraman in it—

SPIKE: The cameramen were outside the cage.

WALTON: Then, suddenly, the shark goes in for the kill. Ooo, look how big the jaws are. He has lots of teeth. Hey, how come sharks always seem like guys? You never think of a shark being a girl. Wouldn't it be bad to be a girl shark? You're so ugly and mean looking. It's amazing that sharks have babies. Who would marry a shark? Who would go on a date with a shark? Sharks in love—gross! Anyhow, no one ever gets killed on these shows. They wouldn't show them on TV if they did. So it's always going to be boring and disappointing. Animals are stupid. They just eat and walk or swim around. Big deal. All animals are boring.

COREY: Are you serious?

WALTON: I said it, didn't I?

SPIKE: So what are you saying, that we're stupid to like sharks?

WALTON: You can like whatever you want. I just think sharks are boring.

ROGER: Would it be boring to have your arm ripped off?

WALTON: No. Not boring. But so what? A shark's not going to rip my arm off.

JIM: It could.

WALTON: I doubt it.

COREY: But it *could*.

WALTON: So?

SPIKE: So only an idiot wouldn't like sharks.

WALTON: What? So I'm an idiot for not liking something that could rip my arm off? That makes a lot of sense.

COREY: It does.

SPIKE: You bet it does, stupid.

WALTON: I think you're the stupid one.

(LISA and POSY enter.)

JIM: You're stupider.

SPIKE: So you're saying I'm stupid, too, but not *as* stupid?

JIM: No, I'm saying he's the stupidest in, like, the world.

WALTON: That's impossible.

ROGER: It's not impossible.

WALTON: Yes, it is.

COREY: Like you would know.

WALTON: Like *you* would know! But there are plenty of people stupider than me. Babies for starters.

SPIKE: You think you know everything.

WALTON: I know more than you.

LISA: How come you're fighting?

JIM: Because.

LISA: That's not an answer.

ROGER: What do you think of sharks?

LISA: Sharks are scary.

COREY: See?

WALTON: But the chances of you running into a shark are practically impossible.

POSY: But that doesn't make them less scary. 'Cause what if I'm the one person who does?

WALTON: People, we live in Kansas!

POSY: So? I went to Florida once.

LISA: So why are you fighting? About sharks?

SPIKE: Walton thinks sharks are boring.

LISA: So why are you fighting?

JIM: Because they're not!

POSY: Yeah, they're not boring. They're too scary to be boring.

LISA: Yeah, but I don't get it. Why would you fight about that?

COREY: Because.

LISA: Posy, do you get this?

POSY: Well, they disagree.

LISA: Yeah, but . . .

POSY: Why are we talking to boys anyway?

LISA: I don't know.

(POSY and LISA exit.)

SPIKE: Even girls think sharks are cool.

WALTON: That's not what they said.

COREY: Well, girls don't make sense.

ROGER: Sure, they do. At least some of the time.

WALTON: No, they never make sense. They just blabber all day.

ROGER: Your mother's a girl.

WALTON: Are you saying something about my mother?

ROGER: No, you are.

SPIKE: Dude, you do not say something about someone's mother.

JIM: That's just stupid.

ROGER: You're saying I'm stupid? 'Cause I'm smarter than you.

JIM: You're not smarter than me.

ROGER: I get better grades.

JIM: I'm street smart.

COREY: Is that what your mom tells you?

JIM: Are you making a crack about my mom?

COREY: Maybe I am!

JIM: You better shut up about my mom.

COREY: What if I don't?

SPIKE: You can't let him get away with that, Jim.

ROGER: You should butt out.

SPIKE: Oh really? Says who?

ROGER: Says me.

> (SPIKE pushes ROGER. ROGER pushes SPIKE. SPIKE bumps into COREY.)

COREY: Hey, watch it!

SPIKE: Who's gonna make me watch it?

COREY: I will.

(COREY pushes SPIKE. MELANIE, VAL, and BELLA enter as the boys' fight goes on.)

JIM: Why don't you mind your own business?

COREY: Why don't *you* mind *your* own business?

JIM: Why should I?

COREY: Because I said so.

JIM: You're stupid.

(JIM pushes COREY. COREY pushes JIM.)

WALTON: Hey, guys?

(JIM pushes WALTON. WALTON pushes SPIKE. SPIKE pushes ROGER.)

ROGER: You're dead.

SPIKE: Not if I kill you first.

ROGER: I dare you.

MELANIE: *(Yelling.)* Stop it! Don't fight. Fighting is bad. Why do boys always fight? Come on, guys. Talk it out. What's the matter? You're all friends. Why are you fighting?

JIM: I dunno. Because.

MELANIE: Because? That's your reason?

COREY: There's a reason.

MELANIE: What is it? What started it?

WALTON: Someone said something about someone's mom.

JIM: Yeah!

SPIKE: Who was it?

WALTON: Does it matter?

ROGER: No.

MELANIE: So you don't even care why you're fighting? Well, that makes a lot of sense.

WALTON: So you know what sense is.

MELANIE: Sure. All girls do.

ROGER: All girls know what sense is? That is funny.

VAL: Don't be insulting. She's trying to help.

JIM: She's butting in.

BELLA: She's being nice, stupid.

JIM: Who are you calling stupid?

BELLA: You.

COREY: It's not fair that we can't fight girls, too.

VAL: Why do you fight at all?

SPIKE: We fight because we're guys. Duh. It's what we do. It's who we are. Girls don't understand because you're like another species. You may as well be sharks or something. You may as well have a fin coming out of your back and five rows of teeth.

VAL: Don't be disgusting.

SPIKE: See? That's not disgusting. I'm just saying you're totally different. We need to blow off some steam. It doesn't mean we're not friends. Roger's not going to go cry if Jim is mad at him or anything. Walton's not going to sulk in the corner for a month if Corey doesn't like his shirt or something. We make sense. We just get it off our chest, do a little pushing, and we're done. It's over. We take care of our problems. It's done quickly and easily. I'm mad, so I hit you. It's that simple. It doesn't go on for weeks and no one takes sides and no one cries. It's how fights are supposed to go.

MELANIE: I don't get it.

BELLA: Boys. They don't make any sense.

Scene 2: Girls

MELANIE: I'm not talking to you.

ROGER: It sounds like you're talking to her.

VAL: Shows what you know.

LISA: Well, I'm not talking to you either!

JIM: There's a lot of talking for people who aren't talking.

BELLA: Why don't you two go away now?

ROGER: Does this mean you're not talking to us?

POSY: We're talking to you.

JIM: Too bad.

(ROGER and JIM exit.)

BELLA: Boys are stupid.

MELANIE: Anyway, as I was saying, I'm not talking to you, Lisa. And you know why.

LISA: I'm not talking to you either, but I don't know why you're not talking to me because I didn't do anything to you.

MELANIE: Well, why would I not be talking to you unless you did something to make me not want to talk to you?

LISA: I don't know. I don't know why you do anything.

POSY: Melanie, you've been mean to Lisa all year. She's just had enough.

MELANIE: Posy, you should butt out. This doesn't concern you.

LISA: See? That's how you treat people. It's not nice. You think you're the boss, and so you boss everyone around all the time. And Val and Bella just go along with whatever you say. I don't know why. But then you think you can treat everyone like that. But you can't. I don't like it, Melanie. I think friendships should be about more than just getting what you want. Like the other day, I wanted to go inside and talk and you wanted to stay outside and you refused to do what I want for once. And there are lots and lots of time when I do what you want. I just can't understand why sometimes you can't let someone else have her way instead. Just every once in a while. It's called compromise.

MELANIE: It was a nice day. Why should I go inside?

LISA: You could have just been nice for once. I thought we were best friends. But then you wouldn't do what I wanted even though I wanted to talk to you. So that hurt my feelings. So I don't think we can be friends anymore.

MELANIE: Fine with me. Posy's your best friend anyway.

LISA: She's *one* of my best friends. And I've known you longer so you should have known that you hurt my feelings.

MELANIE: You shouldn't be so sensitive.

POSY: You shouldn't tell her what to do.

MELANIE: You're butting in again!

POSY: Because you're not being nice!

VAL: Posy, you're just jealous of Melanie since she and Lisa used to be best friends and you wanted to be Lisa's best friend.

POSY: That's not true! We can all be friends. And I'm Lisa's best friend, too, anyhow. She just said so.

BELLA: She's just trying not to make you feel bad. You're just her best friend when Melanie's not around.

POSY: That's not true!

LISA: Shut up, you guys! You don't know what you're talking about.

(SPIKE, JIM, COREY, ROGER, and WALTON enter.)

ROGER: Still not talking? Seems like you spend all day not talking on and on and on and on and on—

VAL: Shut up, Roger.

ROGER: Make me.

VAL: I wish.

ROGER: So do.

COREY: She likes you!

VAL: Don't be disgusting.

ROGER: Yeah. That's disgusting.

VAL: I'm not disgusting, you are!

ROGER: You're completely disgusting.

VAL: You wish!

WALTON: So what are you girls fighting about now?

POSY: You make it sound like we fight all the time.

SPIKE: You do fight all the time. "Look! I'm a girl! I just fight blah blah blah all the time! You're wearing my shirt! You like her best! Blah blah blah!"

BELLA: Do you think that's funny? 'Cause it's not.

SPIKE: 'Cause it is.

BELLA: No, it's not. Go away now. We're having a serious discussion.

JIM: About lipstick?

LISA: We don't wear lipstick.

MELANIE: Gloss maybe.

WALTON: Oooh, gloss. So much better than lipstick.

BELLA: You should shut up now.

MELANIE: Go away.

SPIKE: Fine. It's better than hanging around here.

(SPIKE, JIM, COREY, ROGER, and WALTON exit.)

BELLA: They really don't get it.

VAL: They definitely don't get us.

POSY: They don't get anything.

MELANIE: Let's face it; boys don't make sense.

LISA: Well, we could go inside to talk and get away from them except Melanie won't do that.

MELANIE: I didn't say I won't do that. I said that I didn't want to do that the other day, so I didn't. I don't see why that's so bad. We don't always have to do the same thing.

LISA: But if I don't do what you say, you get mad.

MELANIE: I don't get mad if people don't do what I want. It's your life and a free country and you can do whatever you want. I don't care.

POSY: Maybe you should care if it's your friends.

MELANIE: I really don't get why you're mad, Lisa. I don't have time for a long conversation about it. Get over it.

LISA: Fine. We're not friends any more.

MELANIE: Fine. Then don't talk to me.

LISA: Fine. I won't.

MELANIE: Fine. And don't ask to borrow any of my stuff.

LISA: Fine. I don't care.

MELANIE: Fine. Let's go, Val and Bella.

LISA: Val and Bella, you know you don't have to go with her. All she does is boss you around.

BELLA: We don't *have* to go with her. But she's our friend.

VAL: We want to go with her.

(MELANIE, VAL, and BELLA exit.)

POSY: Don't worry about them. They're creeps.

LISA: But that's just it, Posy, they weren't always creeps. Melanie used to be my best friend.

POSY: I thought I was your best friend.

LISA: You are.

POSY: I'm way nicer to you than Melanie is. She's just bossy and always has to get her way. I listen to you. And we have more in common. I don't know why you'd want to be Melanie's best friend.

LISA: You're right. She's not nice.

POSY: And why be friends with people who aren't nice to you? That goes against the definition of being someone's friend. It doesn't make any sense. So don't worry about Melanie. She's selfish. She only thinks about herself. Who cares if you never talk to her again? You can always talk to me. Whenever you want.

LISA: Thanks, Posy.

POSY: So how come you seem sad?

LISA: I don't know. I just feel kind of sad. Melanie and I were friends for so long. We stood next to each other in choir practice and drew a picture of Mr. Bartlett together in reading class when we were little and got into trouble . . . We've just been friends forever. And I don't know why she changed. It's not the same anymore. She's not the same person. And I'm kind of mad that she's such close friends with Val and Bella. I just don't know what I did. It's like I'm not cool enough to be around her now.

POSY: That just shows how dumb she is.

LISA: I know it's stupid, but it still hurts my feelings a little, Posy. Does that make any sense? I mean, I don't care. I don't need her. I have you. You're my best *best* friend. So it's her loss and all that. I just don't know why she'd be so mean and heartless.

POSY: It's her loss.

LISA: It *is* her loss. I don't care anymore. We're, like, divorced. Unless she apologizes—

POSY: Who even cares if she does? She doesn't deserve to be your friend.

LISA: Well, if she apologizes I'd *consider* being her friend again. It's only fair.

(COREY enters.)

COREY: Lisa, Melanie wants to talk to you.

LISA: Well, I don't want to talk to her.

COREY: She says you should go over and talk to her.

LISA: Why doesn't she come over to me?

COREY: How should I know? I'm only saying what she said. I don't care.

(COREY exits.)

LISA: I guess I should go talk to her.

POSY: She should come over here if she wants to talk to you.

LISA: Maybe she wants to apologize.

POSY: Maybe she should come over here to apologize. She's bossing you around again, Lisa.

LISA: I know. *(Beat.)* But I'd really like to know what she has to say. And . . . we've been friends for a long time. Maybe I should meet her halfway.

POSY: She's just bossing you around again.

LISA: I know . . .

(Beat.)

LISA: I'll be back in a minute.

(LISA exits. POSY sighs.)

TALK BACK!

1. Which way of fighting makes more sense to you: the girls' way or the boys' way? Why?

2. Can you think of another way to solve an argument?

3. Which character is most like you and why?

4. Have you ever grown apart from a friend? What was that like?

5. Have you ever picked a fight with someone? If so, why?

6. Would you rather be friends with someone very similar to you or someone different than you?

7. Do you like arguing or do you hate it? Why?

8. What do you think Lisa should do at the end?

9. Can you think of any reasons why you might want to stop being friends with someone?

10. What really annoys you or makes you angry?

BUCK'S THING

3F, 5M

WHO

FEMALES
Demi
India
Mom

MALES
Buck
George
Jason
Malcolm
Skeet

WHERE Scene 1: School; Scene 2: Buck's house.

WHEN Present day.

🎭 Look at the text carefully. What do your lines say about your character? Does anyone else comment on your behavior? See if you can use this information to build your character.

✎ Use this same title and come up with a completely different play. For example, Buck's "thing" could be something he finds or his little sister. Use your imagination!

Scene 1: Failure!

GEORGE: Hey, Skeet, that drawing is excellent.

SKEET: Thanks. I was just doodling.

BUCK: That really is good. How did you do it?

SKEET: I don't know. Just did it.

BUCK: Yeah, but how?

SKEET: Dunno. Didn't really think about it.

BUCK: Thanks a lot.

GEORGE: What are you mad about, Buck? He doesn't know how he did it. So what?

BUCK: So—

(DEMI and INDIA enter.)

DEMI: What's going on, guys?

SKEET: Nothing. What's going on?

INDIA: We just got done rehearsing for a play we're doing this summer. It's going to be excellent.

DEMI: India and I both sing. It's excellent.

BUCK: How did you know you could sing?

DEMI: What do you mean?

INDIA: You just open your mouth and try.

BUCK: Yeah, but how did you know you were good enough?

DEMI: I don't know. I just like it. And people tell me.

BUCK: No one tells me I'm good at anything.

GEORGE: Maybe you're not good at anything.

INDIA: George! Don't say that! Everybody's good at something.

BUCK: No! George might be right. I'm not good at anything.

DEMI: Come on, Buck. You must be good at something.

BUCK: What? Can anyone think of anything?

INDIA: There must be something.

BUCK: Tell me one thing.

(Beat where everyone looks at each other and tries to think of something to say to BUCK.)

BUCK: See?

GEORGE: Wait! I've got something.

BUCK: What?

(Beat.)

GEORGE: No. I guess everyone can do that.

SKEET: Maybe we just don't know you well enough.

INDIA: Maybe what you're good at just hasn't come up!

GEORGE: Yeah!

BUCK: What do you mean?

INDIA: Well, maybe you're really good at flying an airplane or something. Only you're a kid, and no one's going to let you fly a plane.

GEORGE: Yeah!

BUCK: But I can't even get the DVD player to work. How am I gonna fly a plane?

DEMI: Well, maybe not exactly that. Maybe it's something else.

INDIA: Only something you can't learn in school.

(JASON enters with a trophy.)

JASON: Look, guys! I just won a major award!

SKEET: For what?

JASON: Well, being athletic, perfect attendance, community service, and getting straight A's.

BUCK: I hate you, Jason.

JASON: Hey, little bro, what's the problem?

GEORGE: Buck's not good at anything—anything we know about *yet* anyway.

JASON: You're good at lots of stuff, Buck.

BUCK: Shut up, Jason.

JASON: Why are you mad at me? What did I ever do to you?

BUCK: Why am I mad at you? Oh, let's see. You're just perfect at everything in the entire universe. Look at your award! You're athletic, smart, nice to poor people, never sick—you're practically a superhero. I wouldn't be surprised if you could fly, Jason. Do you know what it's like having a perfect brother? It stinks. It really stinks. Even if I were good at something, no one would know. Because you're *perfect* at everything. And you've taken everything up, too. There's nothing left for me to be good at.

JASON: How is that my fault?

BUCK: It's not your fault exactly. I guess you were born with all the good genes. It's just that you show off too much about it.

JASON: I never show off.

BUCK: Sure you do. Did you *have* to come in here and show my friends your major award?

JASON: I was happy.

BUCK: Maybe next time you should think a little more about people's feelings.

JASON: Maybe you should think about *my* feelings. You're my brother. You should be happy for me.

BUCK: Well, excuse me, but I don't think I can be happy for you. I'll have to leave all the compliments and praise and "oh, you're so perfect Jason" junk to Mom and Dad.

JASON: Jeez, Buck. You're being a real jerk. I guess I'll just get out of your way so you can sit around feeling sorry for yourself.

BUCK: I'm not feeling sorry for myself.

SKEET: Yeah, you kind of are.

BUCK: Thanks a lot. Everyone's against me.

GEORGE: I guess so.

DEMI: George, what's wrong with you? You're agreeing with everyone.

GEORGE: I guess so.

INDIA: We're not against you, Buck. But it's not Jason's fault he's really smart and all that.

BUCK: I know. I didn't say it was.

JASON: Well, whatever. I'm leaving. See you at home.

(JASON exits.)

BUCK: You guys, I just have to find one thing—one little

thing—I'm good at that Jason's not. I have to find *my* thing.

SKEET: Maybe your thing would be being the guy without a "thing." Who says everyone needs a thing? I think that's pointless. Why does everybody have to be good at something? There's nothing wrong with being ordinary. Personally, I'd rather be around people who were just cool and relaxed. I don't care if they're really great in history class or something. I mean who wants to sit around talking about Christopher Columbus? Not me. I'd just rather eat pizza. You can eat pizza, Buck. I've got no problems with you.

BUCK: But you don't have brothers or sisters. That changes everything.

SKEET: I don't have brothers or sisters but, pressure-wise, it can be even worse being an only child. You are your parent's only hope. But no matter what your family's like, you can't let this stuff get you down. Know what? I think you've got it good, actually. Your brother's perfect, right?

BUCK: Right.

SKEET: So you've got no pressure. They've already got the dream child so all the pressure's off you. You should enjoy yourself! Be a slob, Buck!

DEMI: Skeet, you are not helpful.

BUCK: No, wait. He might have a point.

GEORGE: I see his point.

INDIA: Shut up, George.

GEORGE: Whatever you say.

BUCK: So my "thing" is that I'm not good at anything. I'm a slob. I'm a failure. I can be as ordinary as I want. Why try to compete? I can just sit back, watch TV, and eat pizza while Jason works his butt off. Yeah! I think I could like that!

DEMI: No, Buck, don't give up. I'm sure you're good at lots of things.

BUCK: No. I'm not good at anything! I'm good at nothing!

DEMI: Buck . . .

BUCK: No, it's good. I can do this. I can be good at nothing. That's my "thing"!

Scene 2: Winner?

BUCK: What a good day. I've done exactly nothing.

MALCOLM: I love days like this.

BUCK: We've watched some terrible movies, though.

MALCOLM: That's what happens when you do nothing on a Saturday afternoon.

(MOM *enters.*)

MOM: How are you boys doing?

BUCK: Fine, Mom.

MOM: How are you, Malcolm?

MALCOLM: Fine.

MOM: Where are the other boys?

BUCK: Out doing stuff.

MOM: Maybe you boys should go out, too.

BUCK: Nah.

MOM: It's a nice day.

BUCK: Nah.

MOM: Jason's outside.

BUCK: Good for him.

MOM: You and Jason used to do things together outside.

BUCK: That was then, this is now, Mom.

MOM: Sometimes I worry about you, Buck.

BUCK: Don't, Mom. Everything's good. Jason is the good son who plays sports outside on the weekends, and I'm the one who sits in the house and eats pizza.

MOM: Try to get outside sometime today, boys. It's a beautiful day outside.

BUCK: OK, Mom.

(MOM exits.)

BUCK: Sorry about that.

MALCOLM: No problem.

(SKEET and GEORGE enter.)

GEORGE: Hey! We're here.

MALCOLM: It's about time.

BUCK: What have you been doing? Enjoying the fresh air?

SKEET: No way. My mom told me I couldn't leave the house 'til I cleaned my room.

GEORGE: I was sleeping.

MALCOLM: Losers.

GEORGE: What were you doing?

BUCK: Eating.

SKEET: And we're the losers?

MALCOLM: Yeah.

GEORGE: I like sleeping.

SKEET: Dude, how much did you eat?

MALCOLM: I just had about four slices.

SKEET: There's, like, four *boxes* here.

BUCK: Yeah. I ate the rest.

GEORGE: You ate three and a half pizzas?

BUCK: Yeah. I forgot to eat breakfast.

SKEET: So you ate three and a half pizzas?

BUCK: I guess so. I wasn't paying attention.

SKEET: That must be a record!

GEORGE: You're my hero. That is unbelievable.

SKEET: You *are* good at something, Buck. You can eat pizza.

BUCK: What?

GEORGE: Remember that day when you were going on and on about your "thing"? Maybe this is your thing. You know people win money at eating contests and stuff. You could be a millionaire or something!

BUCK: Are you serious?

MALCOLM: That's true. Some Japanese guy ate, like, a million hot dogs in five minutes a few weeks back.

SKEET: Do you like hot dogs?

BUCK: Sure.

GEORGE: Imagine if that was your job in life. Eating. This is blowing my mind. What an amazing job. People could pay you for eating. You'd get all the food your parents don't want you to eat, too. At least all the food my parents hate. Pizza, hot dogs, soda! Last night my mom made grilled eggplant and smoked salmon—it was terrible! I would do anything for a hot dog in my house. And you have the potential, Buck, to eat them every single day *as your job!* Is anyone else excited about this? Am I the only one whose mind is blown? This is amazing! You have to do something with this, Buck. You've got, like, a freakishly stretchy stomach. And it's your duty as an American kid to take advantage of this. You've taken being a slob to a whole new level! You're my hero, Buck.

MALCOLM: Take it easy, George.

GEORGE: Don't you see how great this is?

SKEET: It is pretty great. I wish I could do that.

BUCK: So, I'm good at something? I don't know how I feel about this. I was just getting used to being the guy who was good at nothing. This changes everything. I don't know if I like this. I can feel the pressure already. I mean, what if I let people down? What if I can't really be a competitive eater? What if I fail? Maybe it's better not to try. Then I won't be disappointed again and no one would expect anything from me either.

GEORGE: Yeah, but you have a natural talent, Buck. You can't ignore that.

BUCK: Listen, I just can't do this! This is too much. I'm not ready for this. I was just settling into being a slob. I just stopped worrying about how Jason's perfect and I'm not. I'm starting to train my parents not to expect much from me. Things are starting to go well. I feel relaxed. I'm doing just what I want to do and not worrying about anything else. My life was really starting to be good. And now this? I don't know, guys. I just don't know.

(*JASON enters.*)

JASON: Hey, Mom! I scored the winning goal in the tournament!

(*MOM enters.*)

MOM: Jason, that's fantastic! I'm so proud of you.

JASON: There were three seconds left in the game, too.

MOM: That's amazing!

JASON: A guy came up to me who is a talent scout and said he's going to keep his eye on me. He said he sees great things, maybe even a professional career for me, if I keep it up. Mom, I could be a professional athlete!

MOM: We all believe in you, Jason. Dad will be so happy to hear that when he gets home.

JASON: Well, I'm going to go do my homework.

MOM: You're the best. I'm so proud of you, Jason.

(MOM and JASON exit.)

SKEET: Are you going to let him get away with that?

BUCK: What?

MALCOLM: Dude, your brother is such a loser.

BUCK: What?

MALCOLM: People are supposed to be flawed. He makes me want to puke.

SKEET: Seriously. He's making *me* mad now. You can't let him get away with this. He's making all of us look bad.

BUCK: But I thought I should embrace my slobness. That's what you said. That's what I've been doing!

GEORGE: Maybe it's not a good idea. I mean, you could do awesome things, Buck. You could travel the world with your talent.

BUCK: I have talent. That is so weird to hear.

GEORGE: Face it. You're going to be rich and famous.

SKEET: You have to crush your brother. Forget that other stuff.

MALCOLM: It could be fun. You don't have to learn any complicated math or anything. It's just eating.

(JASON enters.)

JASON: Where's Mom?

BUCK: I don't know.

JASON: Well, when you see her, can you tell her I'm going to go feed the poor. I'll be home for dinner.

(JASON exits.)

SKEET: Come on, Buck.

GEORGE: Come on!

MALCOLM: You can do it!

BUCK: *(Yelling.)* Mom? I need to go to the store and buy twenty packs of hot dogs, OK?

TALK BACK!

1. Are you a competitive person? Why or why not?

2. What are your talents?

3. Can you think of some talents that don't show up in school?

4. Is it possible to have no talents? Why or why not?

5. Buck is envious of his brother Jason. Are you envious of anyone? Why?

6. What talent do you wish you had, but don't? If you could be really, really good at one thing, what would it be?

UNCOOL CAT

5F, 2M

WHO

FEMALES   MALES
   Cat   Ian
   Chloe   Ren
   Mags
   Shannon
   Tribeca

WHERE Scene 1: At school; Scene 2: Tribeca's house.

WHEN Present day.

🎭 Notice how you act with your real friends. For example, do you talk, stand, or act differently around your friends than you do around strangers? Notice any differences and see if you can incorporate these mannerisms in your acting. It should seem like these characters know each other well and are good friends.

✒ The two monologues in Scene 1 were borrowed from my book *The Ultimate Monologue Book for Middle School Actors, Volume 1*. Find a monologue and write a scene around it, filling out the circumstances and adding other characters.

Scene 1: Scaredy Cat

MAGS: So what are we going to do at your party, Tribeca?

TRIBECA: I've got it all planned out. At six, we eat hamburgers and fries. At six-thirty, we eat cake. Oh, and everyone sings "Happy Birthday," of course. At seven, we watch a scary movie and scream our heads off and practically wet ourselves because we won't walk to the bathroom by ourselves because we're afraid of the dark. I'm guessing somewhere in there my stupid brother tries to scare us. Oh, and we eat popcorn during the movie and cheese curls. Then we put on my sister's makeup at nine and paint our fingernails and toes at nine-thirty. What else? We eat ice cream. We tell ghost stories. I know this one about a man who gets killed—I'll tell it later. No sleeping allowed. Oh, and someone barfs. Someone always barfs. I dunno why.

CHLOE: It sounds amazing.

SHANNON: I can't wait.

CAT: Yeah, that will be fun. I guess. Couldn't we watch a comedy? Like *Ace Ventura*? My mom never wants me to watch that. She says it's crude. We could watch that.

TRIBECA: No, it has to be a scary movie.

CAT: I'm not crazy about scary movies. I don't understand why people like to be scared—I hate it! When I was in third grade, in art class, Ellen told me about the movie *The Exorcist* where the devil possesses this girl.

SHANNON: We could see that!

CAT: No! Don't make me see it! What I was going to say is that ever since I *heard* about that movie I stay awake at night, and I think I will be possessed or that my little sister who shares a room with me—which I hate—will be possessed. And I can't decide which is worse. Being possessed myself, or being stuck in the room with a possessed person. I stare at her face in the dark to see if it starts changing. She grinds her teeth when she sleeps so sometimes I think it's happening; she's getting possessed.

MAGS: Oh my God, that is so cool. How can you keep from getting possessed?

CAT: The only way not to get possessed is to be really religious. I hate church so I'm a goner. At the same time, the devil likes to take over girls the most because they aren't as bad as adults. I just can't win! Can we please, please see *Ace Ventura* on Friday?

TRIBECA: No way! We're seeing something scary. And I like the way that movie sounds.

CAT: No! Please!

CHLOE: Why would the devil like to take over girls instead of adults? I don't get it.

CAT: Because it's, like, more of a victory for evil or something. I don't know. Plus, preteens are so confused and stuff, we're maybe more open to it? I don't know. All I know is I do not want to be possessed.

MAGS: It might be fun to be really, really bad. Think about it. If you go to hell, you can do every bad thing you've ever wanted.

SHANNON: But aren't you tortured?

CHLOE: Maybe that's just what they want us to think. You know, like fairy tales.

TRIBECA: What are you talking about?

CHLOE: You know, like *Sleeping Beauty* is supposed to teach us not to be too curious and to do what we're told. If she'd just stayed away from the spindle, she wouldn't be put in that coma.

SHANNON: I forgot about the spindle thing!

MAGS: Yeah, but she also wouldn't have been kissed by the prince.

CAT: You don't know that. It might have happened anyway.

TRIBECA: No, it was fate. It was all fate.

SHANNON: Wait a sec. I just caught onto something. Your mother won't let you see *Ace Ventura?*

CAT: Yeah. So?

SHANNON: So that is so weird!

CAT: She says the humor is vulgar.

CHLOE: *Ace Ventura* is funny.

TRIBECA: Everyone's seen it.

MAGS: I don't see what's so bad about it.

SHANNON: Your mom must be really strict.

CAT: I guess. I mean, I don't get to see as many movies as some other people. But it's not so bad.

SHANNON: Yeah, but *Ace Ventura?* That's like nothing.

TRIBECA: You don't want to see the scary movie because your mom wouldn't like it!

CAT: No, that's not it. I just don't like scary movies. I don't like being scared. I'd rather laugh, that's all.

CHLOE: I love being scared! It's delicious. I love that feeling when you can almost feel the killer coming up behind you. And you hear every little noise. And suddenly everyone around you starts to look suspicious and murderous.

CAT: That's exactly what I hate! How can you like that?

CHLOE: I just do.

MAGS: Everyone does.

CAT: Well, not *everyone* because I don't like it.

TRIBECA: Well, let's take a vote then. Everyone who wants to see a comedy, raise your hand.

(CAT raises her hand.)

CAT: Come on, guys.

TRIBECA: Everyone who wants to see a scary, disgusting horror movie, raise your hand.

(TRIBECA, MAGS, SHANNON, and CHLOE raise their hands.)

CAT: Come on, guys. Please?

TRIBECA: No way. You're outvoted, plus it's my birthday, so I get to pick anyhow. Sorry, Cat.

CAT: Tribeca, please don't be mean.

TRIBECA: I'm not being mean!

SHANNON: It's her birthday.

CHLOE: And you'll be fine. No one's really going to kill you.

MAGS: Or will they? You never really know.

CAT: Mags, stop it! I'm already getting scared.

MAGS: It's the middle of the afternoon! The sun is shining!

CAT: Yeah, but I'm a scaredy cat. I admit it.

TRIBECA: Oh, how cute. And your name is Cat, too.

(REN and IAN enter.)

CAT: Shut up, Beca. It's not cute at all. I know it's stupid, but I can't help it.

REN: Hey, Tribeca, I hear you're having a party.

TRIBECA: I am.

IAN: So where's our invitation?

TRIBECA: No boys. Just girls.

REN: How come?

TRIBECA: Because it's my birthday and I said so.

IAN: Maybe we could just come over for cake.

MAGS: Maybe not.

IAN: Maybe so.

SHANNON: No way! You're just pigs who want free cake.

REN: Well, yeah. Who doesn't want free cake?

CHLOE: But it's her *birthday*.

IAN: So?

CHLOE: So it's not about the cake, it's about it being Tribeca's birthday.

REN: What's the difference?

MAGS: Honestly, you're just too dopey for words.

IAN: Takes one to know one.

SHANNON: Very mature.

REN: So is it a sleepover?

CAT: Yeah.

IAN: Are there going to be pillow fights?

CAT: No.

MAGS: How should we know?

TRIBECA: It's not on the schedule.

SHANNON: And it's none of your business anyway.

IAN: So what's on the "schedule"?

REN: There shouldn't be a schedule at a party.

TRIBECA: Shows what you know.

CHLOE: We're going to watch a movie.

CAT: And eat.

SHANNON: And paint our nails.

MAGS: And tell ghost stories.

IAN: Oooh! Scary stuff!

REN: So you'll be screaming and giggling like morons.

MAGS: No. We wouldn't want to take your job.

SHANNON: Good one, Mags!

MAGS: Thanks, Shannon.

REN: *(Mocking.)* "Good one, Mags!"

IAN: *(Mocking.)* "Thanks so much! Your shirt is so cute!"

REN: *(Mocking.)* "No, yours is!"

IAN: *(Mocking.)* "No, yours!"

CAT: They didn't say that.

CHLOE: And they don't talk like that.

REN: Well, have fun at your little party.

TRIBECA: We will.

MAGS: Mmm, I can't wait to have that cake.

IAN: Who cares? Ren, let's go.

(IAN and REN exit.)

MAGS: It was probably a really good thing that Sleeping Beauty went into her coma thing. She avoided all those years when boys are really stupid and just woke up at the good part.

CAT: I have such a great idea! We could watch *Sleeping Beauty* at your birthday, Tribeca!

TRIBECA: You're kidding, right?

CAT: It could be fun.

TRIBECA: It could be stupid.

CHLOE: That's baby stuff, Cat.

SHANNON: No, we definitely need to watch a horror movie.

TRIBECA: Sorry, Cat. You'll just have to deal.

Scene 2: Kiddy Cat

CHLOE: This is so exciting!

SHANNON: What movie did you get, Beca?

TRIBECA: I got *Blood Lake.* There's these kids in a cabin by the woods with a lake, of course, and they keep getting killed off, of course, by this crazy psychokiller going after them one by one.

MAGS: Of course!

CHLOE: Sounds scary!

CAT: Very scary.

CHLOE: Don't worry, Cat, we won't let you be killed.

CAT: Thanks a lot. If there were a crazy psychokiller, you wouldn't be able to stop him.

SHANNON: If we were all being pursued by a crazy psychokiller, who do you think would be the last girl standing?

CHLOE: I think it would be Tribeca. And I bet I'd get killed first.

CAT: Why?

CHLOE: Tribeca is strong and I'm weak. I'm the slowest runner of all of us. Remember when we had to do that Presidential Challenge fitness thing? When we were doing those stupid shuttle relays, I was, like, ten minutes slower than everyone else. It was so embarrassing.

Everyone was just staring at me running for ages. It was humiliating!

MAGS: I remember that! You looked like you were in slow motion.

CHLOE: Thanks a lot!

SHANNON: I think Mags would go first because she's got the smart mouth. Isn't that what usually happens?

MAGS: But I'm clever. I could outsmart a psychokiller.

SHANNON: But that would be your downfall. You would be too confident.

TRIBECA: If it were a movie, I bet Cat would be the last girl standing since she's so scared.

MAGS: Yeah! And she'd have to keep running and running and screaming and screaming—

CAT: I think I'd rather just be killed quickly.

CHLOE: No, you wouldn't. Not if your life was really in danger.

CAT: I used to lie in bed at night and wonder, "If a killer came into my bedroom, would I rather be facing the door so I could have a chance of escaping or would I rather have my back to the door so I wouldn't be scared and he would just kill me?"

MAGS: I guess that's what you thought when you weren't watching your sister to see if she'd get possessed by the devil.

TRIBECA: You sure think some weird things, Cat.

CAT: I know. I can't help it.

TRIBECA: Oh! Guys! Change of schedule. Instead of eating right away, we're going to listen to music first. My dad is going to pick up the food now, so it won't be here for a while.

SHANNON: Great! What should we listen to?

CHLOE: Since Cat is sad about our movie choice, maybe she should pick the music.

MAGS: What do you think, Tribeca? It's your birthday.

TRIBECA: Fine with me! Cat, the CDs are in the next room.

CAT: OK. If you're sure.

TRIBECA: Sure!

(CAT exits.)

CHLOE: So, do you feel older?

TRIBECA: You know, I don't feel older. I hate that. Do you remember when we would count our half-birthdays and everything? I stopped doing that. And other than having this party, I feel exactly the same as yesterday. I know that I'm not actually a year older, I'm just a day older, but I used to feel really different on my birthday when I was little. It used to be so exciting. But it's just not as . . . big anymore, know what I mean? I guess this is what it feels like to get old. I can't really say that I like it. It's sort of . . . sad.

SHANNON: But you're getting more mature. Isn't that exciting?

TRIBECA: Well, I guess. I'm sort of torn between being excited about, you know, getting closer to being a teen and more mature and being depressed about . . . well, I don't know what I'm depressed about. I just feel a little sad. I guess because when I was immature, I didn't have to worry about anything. Now I feel like I'm going to have to worry about stuff more. Like everything's getting more serious. Know what I mean?

MAGS: I think so. I think I know what you mean, but I don't know how to describe it.

TRIBECA: Me either.

SHANNON: Well, I think you're both crazy. I can't wait to be eighteen and go to college.

TRIBECA: Well, I guess I can't either.

CHLOE: I'm going to go to art college in New York.

TRIBECA: No way! I'm going to be a fashion designer in New York!

CHLOE: We can go together!

SHANNON: But I want to go to California to be a movie director.

TRIBECA: Mags can go with you.

MAGS: No way. I'm going to Harvard to be a lawyer.

CHLOE: I thought you wanted to be a doctor.

SHANNON: I thought you wanted to go to Yale.

MAGS: Well, Harvard or Yale and a doctor or a lawyer. I want to make pots of money.

CHLOE: I'm going to struggle to make ends meet, painting in my funky downtown studio. I'm going to wear a scarf every day.

SHANNON: That's weird.

CHLOE: No, it's not.

(CAT enters.)

CAT: I've got it! The best CD ever! I can't believe you have it! I love this one!

TRIBECA: What is it?

CAT: *Elvis Presley's Greatest Hits.* It's the best music in the universe!

TRIBECA: Oh my God. You're kidding.

CAT: No! You really have it!

TRIBECA: Cat, that's my Dad's CD.

CAT: So?

TRIBECA: So it's completely and totally uncool old people music.

CAT: What? You guys don't like this music?

SHANNON: No way.

CHLOE: Never heard of it.

CAT: What? Have you ever listened to it? It's great!

TRIBECA: Cat, I'm telling you it's massively uncool.

CAT: **Elvis? Uncool? Stop joking with me.**

MAGS: No one is joking, Cat.

CAT: **So you're saying Elvis is dumb. Stupid. Uncool.**

SHANNON: Right.

CAT: **I can't believe this.**

TRIBECA: You're totally embarrassing yourself, Cat. I hate to tell you.

CAT: **Well, I don't *love* . . . I mean, I just have really good memories about this music. It's my dad's favorite, and we'd dance to it all the time when I was little. So . . . I didn't know no one listened to it. I thought . . .**

CHLOE: Why don't you go pick something else.

CAT: **I don't think I can pick another CD, to be honest. I . . . I kind of don't know what else to pick.**

I'll probably pick something else stupid and embarrassing. I don't know who most of the bands are, I guess. I don't really listen to the radio except when my mom's playing it in the car. And she kind of listens to oldie stations. So maybe someone else should pick the music. I didn't know.

TRIBECA: It doesn't matter. I'll do it.

(TRIBECA exits.)

CAT: I'm really embarrassed. I'm really sorry. I didn't know that . . . I feel really dumb.

MAGS: Well, don't. Whatever. It doesn't matter.

CAT: No. Maybe I should go. I bring you guys down. I don't like the movies you like, and I don't know what music you listen to—I just don't fit in. So I'll call my mom and go home. You'll have more fun without me. And let's face it, I was going to have a miserable night. I'd be up all night worrying about who was going to kill me like a little baby. I can't handle horror movies. I really can't. So I guess I'm just a loser. So I'll go home now.

CHLOE: No, don't go!

(TRIBECA reenters.)

TRIBECA: What's going on?

SHANNON: Cat says she wants to go home.

TRIBECA: You can't go home.

CAT: I think I should.

MAGS: You can't. We won't let you.

CAT: I wouldn't have a good time anyway. And I'd spoil your fun.

TRIBECA: Why wouldn't you have a good time?

CAT: Because I don't like to do what you guys do.

CHLOE: So?

TRIBECA: Well, if you think we're not fun then maybe you should go.

CAT: I didn't mean it like that.

TRIBECA: Well, I'm sorry that it's *my* birthday so we're doing what *I* want and not what you want. But you can't always get your way, Cat. The world doesn't revolve around you.

CAT: I didn't say that.

TRIBECA: Well, that's what it sounded like. So maybe you should go home.

CAT: Well, OK. I don't want to ruin things.

CHLOE: Come on, we don't need to fight.

SHANNON: Let's just have fun.

MAGS: Come on, stay, Cat.

CAT: No, Tribeca wants me to go.

TRIBECA: No, *you* want to go, Cat, since we're not going to do everything *you* want.

CAT: Fine.

(*CAT exits.*)

TRIBECA: The food will be here any minute. Then we can have a *good* time.

TALK BACK!

1. Should Cat have stayed? Why or why not?

2. Is Tribeca right to be mad? Why or why not?

3. Why do you think people like to be scared?

4. Do you like to be scared? Why or why not?

5. Do you think Cat is normal or a dork? Why or why not?

6. What scares you?

7. Are you excited or worried about getting older or both? What interests you or concerns you about going into your teen years?

APPENDIX

CHARACTER QUESTIONNAIRE FOR ACTORS

Fill in the following questionnaire as if you are your character. Make up anything you don't know.

PART 1: The Facts

NAME:

AGE/BIRTHDATE:

HEIGHT:

WEIGHT:

HAIR COLOR:

EYE COLOR:

CITY/STATE/COUNTRY YOU LIVE IN:

GRADE*:

BROTHERS/SISTERS:

PARENTS:

UPBRINGING (strict, indifferent, permissive, etc.):

---

* If you are an adult, what educational level did you reach (college, medical school, high school, etc.)?

PART 2: Rate Yourself

On a scale of 1 to 10 (circle one: 10 = great, 1 = bad), rate your:

APPEARANCE	1 2 3 4 5 6 7 8 9 10
IQ	1 2 3 4 5 6 7 8 9 10
SENSE OF HUMOR	1 2 3 4 5 6 7 8 9 10
ATHLETICISM	1 2 3 4 5 6 7 8 9 10
ENTHUSIASM	1 2 3 4 5 6 7 8 9 10
CONFIDENCE	1 2 3 4 5 6 7 8 9 10
DETERMINATION	1 2 3 4 5 6 7 8 9 10
FRIENDLINESS	1 2 3 4 5 6 7 8 9 10
ARTISTICNESS	1 2 3 4 5 6 7 8 9 10

Do you like yourself?	YES	NO
Do you like your family?	YES	NO
Do you like the opposite sex?	YES	NO
Do you like most people you meet?	YES	NO

Which of the following are important to you and which are not? Circle one.

WEALTH	Important	Not Important
KNOWLEDGE	Important	Not Important
POWER	Important	Not Important
PEACE	Important	Not Important
POPULARITY	Important	Not Important
LIKABILITY	Important	Not Important
LOVE	Important	Not Important
SPIRITUALITY/RELIGION	Important	Not Important

PART 3: Favorites

List your favorites (be specific).

FOOD:

SONG:

BOOK:

MOVIE:

TV SHOW:

CITY:

SEASON:

COLOR:

PIECE OF CLOTHING:

SMELL:

ANIMAL:

SOUND:

SCHOOL SUBJECT:

PLACE:

PERSON (historical or living):

PART 4: Describe Yourself

Circle all words/phrases that apply to you:

SHY	OUTGOING
OUTDOOR TYPE	INDOOR TYPE
POSITIVE	NEGATIVE
PARTY PERSON	COUCH POTATO
HOMEBODY	LEADER
FOLLOWER	MOODY
CALM	SILLY
HAPPY	SAD
RELAXED	ENERGETIC
INTELLECTUAL	CLEVER
NEAT	MESSY
FUNNY	HONEST
SNEAKY	DISHONEST
OPEN-MINDED	JUDGMENTAL
CARING	CREATIVE
PRACTICAL	WILD
CAREFUL	WELL-LIKED
ARTISTIC	LAZY
OPINIONATED	IMAGINATIVE
REALISTIC	DRAMATIC
STREETWISE	TOLERANT
HARD-WORKING	SPONTANEOUS
STRONG	BRAVE
CURIOUS	QUIET
CHATTY	DARK
SUNNY	DISAPPOINTING
HOPEFUL	UNDERSTANDING
KIND	BORED
DIFFICULT	COMPLICATED
SWEET	POWERFUL
MACHO	ENTHUSIASTIC
GIRLY	INSECURE
LUCKY	PICKY
DISADVANTAGED	FRIENDLY
GOSSIPY	ANGRY
SECRETIVE	WISHY-WASHY
INDEPENDENT	GEEKY
WEAK	COOL
NURTURING	ANNOYING
REBELLIOUS	GOOD

PART 5: Truth/Dreams

If I die tomorrow, people will remember me as a:

One thing that really annoys me is:

My worst habit is:

I'm really scared of:

My parents think I'm:

When I grow up, I want to be*:

Superpower I'd most like to have:

The thing I'd most like to change about myself is:

My greatest talent is:

I'd most like to travel to:

Three professions I'd like to try:

The title for the story of my life would be:

* If your character is an adult, what is your character's job and does he or she enjoy it?

PLAYWRIGHT'S CHECKLIST

Does my play have:

☐ Conflict?

If everyone gets along, not much happens! It's important to have conflict in any play, comedy, or drama.

☐ Character development?

Do the characters change at all in the course of the play for better or worse? It's interesting to the audience to see some variety in character. We all act differently in different situations, so it makes sense for a character to become more complex when he or she is faced with conflicts.

☐ Plot twists?

What could be more exciting than being surprised by a plot twist you hadn't expected?

☐ Believable dialogue?

Even if the characters are strange and out-of-this-world, make sure the dialogue sounds something like the way people actually speak to one another. Any character voices you create must remain consistent throughout. For example, if a character is very intellectual and proper, having them say "I ain't gonna go" is going to seem very out of place.

☐ **A strong sense of place and time?**

Especially when you don't have a big set and costumes, it's important to make the play's setting clear.

☐ **Characters you can relate to?**

Every play has at least one character the audience can understand and sympathize with. A good way to create conflict is to put this "normal" character in the path of another character that is odd, otherworldly, or downright horrible!

SCENE ELEMENTS WORKSHEET

Answer these questions for each scene you do.

WHO: (Who are you?)

WHERE: (Where are you?)

WHEN: (Is this the past, present, or future? Day or night?)

WHY: (Why are you where you are?)

OBJECTIVE: (What do you want?)

ACTIONS: (What do you do to get what you want? For example, beg, flatter, pressure, and so on.)

CHARACTER TRAITS: (What are you like as a person?)

RELATIONSHIP: (What are your relationships to the other characters?)

OBSTACLES: (What or who stands in the way of your objective?)

EXPLORATION GAMES

Draw a picture of your character(s).

Improvise a scene before the play begins or after it ends.

Dress as your character(s) to see how it changes your behavior.

Make the scene or play into a musical or an opera.

Listen closely to everyone around you during a scene.

Try to make your acting partners respond to your behavior.

Lead with a different body part: in other words, change which part of your body enters the room first and pulls you forward when you walk. Leading with your nose can make you seem pompous, leading with the top of your head can make you seem insecure, etc.

Change the speed/rhythm at which you speak or move.

Decide who you like and who you don't like in the scene; don't be afraid to show it.

Change your volume (whisper or speak out loudly).

Make your voice higher or lower in pitch.

Notice who's taller and who's shorter than you in the scene; let this affect you.

Change your accent.

Sit down with another actor to make up your characters' past lives together.

Do an activity you think your character might do.

Do a chore around the house the way your character might do it.

Write a diary entry, a letter of complaint, or a personal ad as your character.

Come up with a gesture that your character does habitually.

THE AUTHOR

Kristen Dabrowski is an actress, writer, acting teacher, and director. She received her MFA from The Oxford School of Drama in Oxford, England. The actor's life has taken her all over the United States and England. Her other books, published by Smith and Kraus, include *111 Monologues for Middle School Actors Volume 1, The Ultimate Audition Book for Teens 3, 20 Ten-Minute Plays for Teens,* and the *Teens Speak* series. Currently, she lives in the world's smallest apartment in New York City. You can contact the author at monologue madness@yahoo.com.